Scenario Development for the 2015 Quadrennial Energy Review

Assessing Stresses, Opportunities, and Resilience in the Transmission, Storage, and Distribution Systems for Oil, and Refined-Oil Products, Electricity, and Natural Gas

Keith Crane, Debra Knopman, Nicholas Burger, Anu Narayanan, James D. Powers, Henry H. Willis

For more information on this publication, visit www.rand.org/t/RR1286

DISCLAIMER: This work was performed in part under funding from DOE/Office of Energy Policy and Systems Analysis under DOE/National Energy Technology Laboratory contract (FE0004002) with subcontract to RAND. This report was prepared as an account of work sponsored by an agency of the United States Government. Neither the United States Government nor any agency thereof, nor any of their employees, makes any warranty, express or implied, or assumes any legal liability or responsibility for the accuracy, completeness, or usefulness of any information, apparatus, product, or process disclosed, or represents that its use would not infringe privately owned rights. Reference herein to any specific commercial product, process, or service by trade name, trademark, manufacturer, or otherwise does not necessarily constitute or imply its endorsement, recommendation, or favoring by the United States Government or any agency thereof. The views and opinions of authors expressed herein do not necessarily state or reflect those of the United States Government or any agency thereof.

Library of Congress Cataloging-in-Publication Data is available for this publication.
ISBN: 978-0-8330-9559-6

Published by the RAND Corporation, Santa Monica, Calif.
© Copyright 2016 RAND Corporation
RAND® is a registered trademark.

Cover image: iStock/kokouu

Support RAND
Make a tax-deductible charitable contribution at
www.rand.org/giving/contribute

www.rand.org

Preface

This report describes an analytical framework and associated metrics for examining future opportunities, vulnerabilities, and risks for the next 15 years to the U.S. energy transmission, storage, and distribution (TS&D) systems under a range of uncertain factors. This work is in support of the 2015 Quadrennial Energy Review (QER), which is focused on TS&D systems. Its purpose is to help our sponsor, the U.S. Department of Energy Office of Energy Policy and Systems Analysis (EPSA), assess how the TS&D systems will perform under high-stress scenarios, in which major shifts in energy demand, supply, or other uncertain factors have the potential to dramatically change the U.S. energy system. The results should lend insight to the formulation of policy responses and investment decisions intended to address challenges and opportunities.

The audience for this report includes energy decisionmakers and analysts in the public and private sectors, legislative staff at the federal and state levels, and others interested in energy policy and security. Other recent RAND publications on related topics include the following:

- Henry H. Willis and Kathleen Loa, *Measuring the Resilience of Energy Distribution Systems*, Santa Monica, Calif.: RAND Corporation, RR-883-DOE, 2015
- Christopher Guo, Craig Bond, and Anu Narayanan, *The Adoption of New Smart-Grid Technologies: Incentives, Outcomes, and Opportunities*, Santa Monica, Calif.: RAND Corporation, RR-717-EMKF, 2015
- Keith Crane, Andreas Goldthau, Michael Toman, Thomas Light, Stuart E. Johnson, Alireza Nader, Angel Rabasa, and Harun Dogo, *Imported Oil and U.S. National Security*, Santa Monica, Calif.: RAND Corporation, MG-838-USCC, 2009.

RAND Infrastructure Resilience and Environmental Policy Program

The research reported here was conducted within the RAND Environment, Energy, and Economic Development Program. Since the development of the report, RAND has evolved this program into the Infrastructure Resilience and Environmental Policy (IREP) program. IREP performs analyses on urbanization and other stresses. This includes research on infrastructure development; infrastructure financing; energy policy; urban planning and the role of public–private partnerships; transportation policy; climate response, mitigation, and adaptation; environmental sustainability; and water resource management and coastal protection. Program research is supported by government agencies, foundations, and the private sector.

This program is part of RAND Justice, Infrastructure, and Environment, a division of the RAND Corporation dedicated to improving policy- and decisionmaking in a wide range of policy domains, including civil and criminal justice, infrastructure protection and homeland security, transportation and energy policy, and environmental and natural resource policy.

Questions or comments about this report should be sent to the project leader, Nicholas Burger (Nicholas_Burger@rand.org). For more information about RAND Infrastructure Resilience and Environmental Policy, see www.rand.org/jie/irep or contact the director at irep@rand.org.

Contents

Preface iii

Figures and Tables vii

Summary ix

Acknowledgments xvii

Abbreviations xix

CHAPTER ONE

Introduction 1

Purpose 1

Approach 1

Organization of This Report 4

CHAPTER TWO

Petroleum and Refined-Oil Products 5

Key Issues 6

Performance Metrics 8

Models and Data 8

Key Uncertainties 8

Policy Options 9

Scenario Analysis 9

Resilience 17

Key Findings 19

CHAPTER THREE

Electric Power 21

Key Issues 22

Performance Metrics 23

Model and Data 23

Key Uncertainties 23

Policy Options 29

Scenario Analysis 29

Resilience 39

Key Findings 42

CHAPTER FOUR
Natural Gas 43
Key Issues 44
Performance Metrics 44
Model and Data 44
Key Uncertainties 44
Scenario Analysis 45
Key Findings 48

CHAPTER FIVE
Implications for Energy Investments and Policy 49
Petroleum and Refined-Oil Products 49
Electric Power 50
Natural Gas 50

APPENDIXES
A. **Models Used to Generate Results** 53
B. **Development of the RAND Low Consumption Case for Oil and Refined Products** 55
C. **Model Output for Electricity for 2050** 57

Bibliography 61

Figures and Tables

Figures

1.1.   Conceptual Diagram of the Robust Decision Making Process 2
2.1.   Historical and Projected U.S. Production of Crude Oil and Consumption of
       Petroleum and Other Liquids 5
2.2.   Petroleum Administration for Defense Districts 7
2.3.   U.S. Consumption of Petroleum and Other Liquids 10
2.4.   Consumption of Petroleum and Other Liquids, 2030, by Petroleum Administration
       for Defense District 11
2.5.   Major Crude Rail Routes from Petroleum Administration for Defense District 2
       West to the East Coast, Gulf Coast, and West Coast 12
2.6.   Oil-Spill Volume per Billion Ton-Miles 16
3.1.   Historical and Projected U.S. Consumption of Electricity, 2011–2030 21
3.2.   Projected Cumulative Retirements of Coal-Fired Generating Capacity, 2012–2040 22
3.3.   North American Electric Reliability Corporation Region Map 26
3.4.   Percentage Changes in Transmission Capacity, by Scenario, 2010 and 2030 30
3.5.   Additional Installed Transmission Capacity, by Scenario, 2010 and 2030 31
3.6.   U.S. Transmission Capacity, by Region and Scenario, 2030 32
3.7.   Additions to U.S. Transmission Capacity, by Region and Scenario, 2030 33
3.8.   Comparison of Transmission Capacity Between the Low Wind Cost and Low Solar
       Cost Scenarios, 2030 34
3.9.   Comparison of Total Transmission Build-Outs Between the Low Wind Cost and
       Low Solar Cost Scenarios, by Originating Region, 2030 34
3.10. Comparison of Transmission Build-Outs Between the Low Wind Cost and Low
       Solar Cost Scenarios Only Within Regions, 2030 35
3.11. Comparison of Greenhouse-Gas Emissions in the Power Sector Among the Base
       Case, the Greenhouse-Gas Emission Cap + Reduced Demand Scenario, and High
       Renewable-Energy Penetration + Reduced Demand Scenario 36
3.12. Comparison of Greenhouse-Gas Emissions and Electricity Prices Across All
       Scenarios to 2030 37
3.13. Comparison of Electricity Prices Across All Scenarios to 2030 38
3.14. Installed Storage Capacity in 2030 40
4.1.   U.S. Gross Withdrawals of Natural Gas, 1967 to 2013 43
4.2.   Total Pipeline Capacity Additions, 2015 to 2030 46
4.3.   National Natural Gas Pipeline Capacity Utilization Rates, 2015 to 2030 47
C.1.   Total U.S. Transmission Capacity, by Scenario, 2050 57
C.2.   Total U.S. Transmission Capacity, by Region and Scenario, 2050 58
C.3.   Transmission Capacity Additions Under Renewable-Resource Cost Scenarios 58

C.4.   Comparison of Transmission Build-Outs Between the Low Cost Wind and Low
        Cost Solar Scenarios, by Region, 2050...59
C.5.   Comparison of Average Electricity Prices Across All Scenarios, 2050 60

Tables

2.1.   Scenarios for Analysis 11
2.2.   Office of Energy Policy and Systems Analysis and IHS Projections Through 2030 of
        New Pipeline Capacity and Costs 15
3.1.   Scenarios Generated from Regional Energy Deployment System Model Runs........... 24
3.2.   Base-Case Outputs 27
4.1.   Natural Gas Scenarios.. 45
A.1.   Models Used to Generate Results.. 54

Summary

Purpose

The purpose of this analysis is to help the U.S. Department of Energy Office of Energy Policy and Systems Analysis (EPSA) assess how energy transmission, storage, and distribution (TS&D) systems might perform under high-stress scenarios in which major shifts in energy demand, supply, or other uncertain factors have the potential to dramatically change the U.S. energy system by 2030. RAND researchers developed an analytical framework and associated metrics for examining vulnerabilities, opportunities, and risks to U.S. TS&D systems through 2030 under a range of uncertainties. We assess major stresses on and opportunities in three major TS&D systems: oil and refined-oil products, electric power, and natural gas. Separately, we also consider the resilience of these systems to short-term shocks and disruptions. EPSA requested this analysis to support the 2015 Quadrennial Energy Review (QER). The QER, which focuses on energy TS&D systems in this first volume, is a federal government initiative to systematically examine energy system performance and explore options to improve that performance to address 21st-century objectives.

Approach

This analysis takes an empirical approach to developing scenarios that could plausibly stress TS&D systems within the time horizon of 2030. By *empirical*, we mean that we identified these stressing scenarios *after* we considered effects of varying key assumptions by one stress factor at a time, relative to a base case, and then examined system performance along a selected set of metrics. This approach is in contrast to selecting scenarios a priori without having first done an initial exploratory analysis to identify the key uncertain factors of interest. This approach is particularly useful when the probabilities of future uncertain events or key changes in TS&D systems cannot be easily quantified. To provide an analytical basis for selecting scenarios of interest for the QER, we examined different sets of assumptions regarding future supply and demand to explore uncertainties applicable to the TS&D systems examined, and we used a concise set of practical metrics to describe U.S. energy TS&D systems' performance and vulnerabilities. To be consistent with the QER, we conducted all analyses of scenarios with models that others developed. In Appendix A, we provide details on the models.

We assume that the Reference scenario for each of the TS&D systems was the Reference case from the 2014 Annual Energy Outlook (U.S. Energy Information Administration [EIA], 2014a). We then explore a set of key uncertain factors intended to expose vulnerabilities and opportunities associated with TS&D systems, relative to the Reference scenario, under assumptions of current policy, as well as other selected policy options through 2030. We also explore combinations of uncertain factors that could reveal potential long-term vulnerabilities and opportunities within each TS&D system. We then use the outputs of the exploratory analysis to identify stressing scenarios under various assumptions about the future and future policy choices. Finally, we discuss, in qualitative terms, the resilience of TS&D systems under selected disruptive events.

Petroleum and Refined-Oil Products

Over the past several years, trends starting in the 1970s in U.S. crude-oil and refined-oil product markets have reversed: U.S. consumption of refined-oil products and natural gas liquids is down, while production has risen. In 2014, consumption had fallen to 8 percent below its peak in 2006, while U.S. crude-oil production had risen sharply. These two changes have driven and will likely continue to drive changes in petroleum and refined-oil product TS&D systems.

Performance Metrics
Consistently with the focus of the EPSA team, the RAND team focused on the following performance metrics to evaluate the performance of domestic TS&D systems for crude-oil and refined-oil products under different production, consumption, and policy conditions:

- reliability: the degree to which available transport and storage capacity can consistently manage interregional flows by volume from producing areas to consuming areas
- affordability: comparative costs of transporting oil per barrel per 1,000 miles by alternative mode between regions
- sustainability: comparative greenhouse-gas (GHG) emissions of transporting oil per barrel per 1,000 miles by alternative mode between regions
- transport safety: comparative numbers of barrels of oil spilled per 1,000 barrels per 1,000 miles by alternative mode between regions.

Scenario Analysis
We identified three factors that, relative to conditions in 2014, have the potential to substantially stress the current level of performance of the TS&D system for crude-oil and refined-oil products:

- continued large increases in crude-oil production
- steep reductions in refined-oil product demand
- eliminating the U.S. legal ban on exports of crude oil.

We distinguish these longer-term stress factors from short-duration shocks, such as a major oil spill from a rail accident or a short-term refinery closure from a hurricane. We did not draw on system models to estimate performance in response to short-duration shocks, but we do discuss the implications of these shocks in qualitative terms in the context of resilience of the TS&D systems.

We drew on EPSA analyses that used the 2014 Annual Energy Outlook (AEO2014) Reference and High Resource oil output cases and that employed the Ponderosa Crude Flow

Model (see Ponderosa Advisors, undated) and Oak Ridge National Laboratory (ORNL) Total Risk Integrated Model (TRIM) for their analyses and projections. We developed our own RAND Low Consumption case, described below and in Appendix B, to explore a wider range of stresses on the system.

Key Findings

- Recent increases in crude-oil output from the Bakken formation, Williston Basin, and Eagle Ford shale have put pressure on the U.S. TS&D system for crude oil, especially railroads moving crude oil out of the Bakken area to the East Coast.
- Under most scenarios, currently planned additions to pipeline capacity, coupled with existing use of rail, should be sufficient to handle projected increases in output. However, in the High Resource case with a continued ban on exports, a combination of lack of demand for tight light crude and constraints on railroad capacity could lead to shutting in some production.
- In the event that the ban on U.S. exports of crude oil is lifted, transportation patterns would shift. Crude oil from the Eagle Ford and Permian basins in Texas would likely be exported; crude from the Williston Basin in North Dakota would be shipped south to refineries on the Gulf of Mexico in lieu of tight light oil from Texas. Current transport of this crude by rail to the East Coast would fall.
- The very large cost differentials between hauling crude via rail versus pipeline (two or three times) will lead to continued expansion in crude-oil pipeline capacity. However, differences in projections of future capacity are large, with the highest projected increase in capacity for the United States running 50 percent more than the alternative.
- Large-scale use of rail to transport crude oil is likely here to stay because of the flexibility that rail provides.
- Competing analyses of GHG emissions associated with rail versus pipeline come up with different results.
- Spillage is generally lower when transporting oil by rail than by pipeline, but several high-profile incidents have raised public concern about transport by rail.
- In the event of another major derailment, especially one involving loss of life, government authorities could impose a moratorium on all rail shipments until safety procedures were reviewed and improved. As long as such a moratorium is in place, it would severely affect production in the Bakken.

Implications for Resilience

The crude-oil and refined-oil product TS&D systems are robust in the face of disruptive events. Even in the event of substantial damage to the system, such as an earthquake in southern California or terrorist attack that would severely damage refineries and import terminals in that region, supplies would flow relatively soon after the event, albeit at a cost in terms of higher prices at the pump (Meade and Molander, 2006).

Electric Power

Substantial amounts of U.S. coal-fired electric power–generating capacity might be retired by 2030 (Federal Energy Regulatory Commission, 2015). Large amounts of nuclear capacity could be retired as well. Continuing to satisfy demand for electric power in the face of potential capacity retirements in a manner that ensures affordable, reliable power in an environmentally sound way is a key challenge facing the electric power–transmission and distribution system. Specifically, we focused on the implications of reductions in generating capacity on demand for bulk and additional feeder transmission capacity and consequent effects on the cost of power on a regional basis. To assess the potential extent of the challenge that these developments pose for the TS&D system, we worked with EPSA to assess potential major shifts in supply caused by changes in power-generating technologies and capacity and shifts in demand for power within the United States through 2030.

Performance Metrics

We examined performance of the electricity TS&D system in terms of three metrics selected as illustrative, although by no means inclusive of all aspects of performance:

- transmission: demand for new transmission
- affordability: changes in retail electric power prices by region stemming from changes in costs of expanding the transmission system and additional generation capacity in response to changes in generation mix
- sustainability: comparative GHG emissions under various futures.

Scenario Analysis

To understand the dynamics of TS&D systems for electric power, we used the Regional Energy Deployment System (ReEDS) model that the National Renewable Energy Laboratory (NREL) developed. We worked with NREL to model a base case guided by the EIA AEO2014 Reference case assumptions that included substantial retirement of coal plants based on existing environmental regulations. NREL ran the ReEDS model using different sets of assumptions corresponding to ten scenarios that we identified to illustrate potential major stresses or opportunities for the TS&D system relative to the 2014 base case. The stress scenarios considered the following factors individually and in combination:

- low and high demand
- cap on GHG emissions (which led to a higher rate of retirement of coal plants than in the base case)
- high market penetration of distributed photovoltaics (DPV)
- low and high natural gas prices
- low wind and solar costs
- high rate of retirement of nuclear plants.

Key Findings

- The ReEDS model represents the bulk and feeder transmission system and thus has some limitations on its ability to estimate whole-system transmission needs. However, in approximate terms, the United States by 2030 might need to increase megawatt-miles (MW-miles) of bulk and feeder transmission capacity by between 5 and 13 percent above current capacity.
- By 2050, a delayed build-out of transmission capacity is projected under the Greenhouse-Gas Emission Cap + High Renewables + Reduced Demand scenario, and the lowest

expansion occurs in the High Renewables + Reduced Demand scenario. Even with less demand than in the base case, the GHG cap forces more transmission to regions where coal-fired plants are retired. Greater intermittent renewable capacity imposes higher demand for transmission lines.

- Total costs of new installed transmission capacity are estimated to be $23.1 billion ($1.2 billion per year) in the base case and as high as $55.5 billion ($2.8 billion per year) in the worst scenario (Greenhouse-Gas Emission Cap + Nuclear Retirements + High Natural Gas Prices scenario). These estimates do not include the cost of investments to improve the reliability of the current transmission system nor additions to intraregional transmission lines that are not tied to renewable-energy production.

- The projected new capacity additions do not exceed recent historical capacity additions. In 2010, the United States installed approximately $10 billion of new capacity, with annual amounts ranging from $3 billion to $13 billion over the past decade.[1]

- A 40-percent reduction of economy-wide GHG emissions from 2013 emission levels, is associated with a 5-percent or $0.005-per-kilowatt-hour increase in electricity prices for the High Demand cases from the base case. If demand falls as in the Low Demand case, electricity prices do not rise.

- Overall, expected transmission capacity additions in the ReEDS model runs are not associated with increases in electricity prices that are significantly different from recent historical changes or predicted increases from other recent modeling efforts. As with all such projections, these results depend on assumptions about the relative costs of alternative sources and, in particular, the rate at which the costs of renewable electricity falls.

Implications for Resilience

We make a distinction between what we call slow-moving–stress cases caused by changes in supply, demand, and cost and major but short-term system-scale disruptions. It is in these later cases that the concept of resilience is particularly relevant in assessing the performance of the TS&D systems. Extreme weather events, operator errors, premeditated physical or cyberattacks, and other disruptions lead to power outages of varying severity. Recovery times for local outages are typically on the order of minutes or hours, although some areas do experience outages of one or more days; at the national scale, the effects tend to be small. Utilities and public service commissions balance the costs of measures to reduce outages against the expected value of reductions in outages.

Long-duration outages over large geographic areas are much less frequent than local outages, but, when they do occur, they have serious impacts. Some events could disrupt the entire U.S. grid, potentially inflicting huge economic losses and disrupting critical services that depend on electricity (Council of Economic Advisers and U.S. Department of Energy Office of Electricity Delivery and Energy Reliability, 2013). A severe geomagnetic storm (from, for example, a solar storm) could induce large current flows that might severely damage high-voltage transformers, leading to voltage collapse, resulting in a nationwide power outage. A

---

[1] ReEDS models only two-fifths of the transmission system (in 2010, 82.2 million MW-miles, a unit that represents a transmission line rated with a carrying capacity of 1 megawatt of power and a 1-mile extent) out of a total system of 200 million MW-miles (U.S. Department of Energy, 2015c, Chapter 3, p. 52). However, the projections of $1.2 billion to $2.8 billion in annual capacity are only 12 to 28 percent of total expenditures on new transmission in 2010, substantially less than the share of the modeled transmission in the total transmission system.

targeted cyberattack on the entire U.S. grid could potentially lead to the same outcome. Steps can be taken to protect the grid from solar storms or cyberattacks, but the necessary technologies tend to be costly, and the actual risk is poorly understood. Other options applicable to outages of all types, but especially suited for widespread and long-duration blackouts, are available, such as microgrids that can be isolated from the larger grid, although actual costs of these measures are not well-established as yet. Utilities and public service commissions often debate approval of such measures because their value to ratepayers can be difficult to reconcile in the context of low-frequency, disruptive events and because the regulators might not always have the technical expertise to assess the prudence of investments that could make systems more resilient. Federal guidance on valuable resilience-enhancing measures could potentially accelerate deployment.

Natural Gas

Natural gas production in the United States has risen sharply, with annual production approximately 35 percent higher in 2014 than in 2005. These production increases are expected to continue. For example, in the EIA AEO2014 High Resource case, natural gas production could reach 34 trillion cubic feet (Tcf) annually by 2030, an increase of 43 percent over 2012 levels of 24 Tcf. To collect, transport, and distribute this increased natural gas production, the U.S. TS&D system will have to be expanded.

The extent of pipeline capacity expansion will depend on the amount of gas produced, its location, and the locations where gas supplies are consumed. In a future in which the U.S. government facilitates exports of sizable amounts of liquefied natural gas (LNG), increased pipeline capacity would be needed to move gas to exporting regions, primarily the Gulf Coast but also the East Coast and coastal Canada. If lower natural gas prices drive continued increases in consumption, different configurations of pipelines could be needed to move supplies to demand centers.

Performance Metric
We sought to identify conditions that have the greatest potential to stress the natural gas TS&D system. Our analysis focused on the single metric of the cost of pipeline expansion. We considered other metrics related to safety and industrial base capacity, but they did not result in discernible changes from current conditions. The model also indicated that the natural gas storage system would not be stressed under the scenarios examined.

Scenario Analysis
We worked with EPSA to develop and analyze results from a small set of natural gas–sector modeling runs, which Deloitte MarketPoint carried out using its World Gas model. The natural gas scenarios enabled analysis of potential stresses on the U.S. natural gas TS&D system—in particular, the potential need for and cost of new pipeline capacity in the context of differ-

ing levels of consumption and prices among plausible futures. We looked at the scenarios that varied the following factors:

- U.S. demand for natural gas
- exports of LNG
- global demand for natural gas.

Key Findings

- Additional demand for natural gas pipelines under all scenarios is modest, less than recent additions.
- Increased capacity utilization plays a key role in mitigating demand for new pipelines.
- The ability to reverse pipeline flows plays a role in decreasing new pipeline construction as sources of supply and demand shift.
- In all of the scenarios examined, normal pipeline expansion and construction practices should be adequate to meet the demand for new pipeline.
- With modest demand for new pipeline capacity, we foresee few pressures that would increase the cost of building pipelines.

Implications for Energy Investments and Policy

The analysis above indicates that potential future stresses on the various TS&D systems examined in this analysis will be regional in nature. The most-immediate stress is on the railroads that transport oil out of the Bakken, Eagle Ford, and Permian basins. Pipelines are being built in these basins to link them to the mid-American pipeline systems that serve the Midwest and South Central United States. However, in the interim, large volumes of oil are being transported by rail, causing substantial congestion on rail systems in those regions. To reduce this congestion, additional pipelines will be needed to move oil out of these basins, connecting them more fully to the midcontinent system. Under a scenario of continued large increases in oil output from North Dakota and Montana and a continued ban on U.S. exports of crude oil, the economic case for building a pipeline from the middle of the United States to East Coast refineries would be strong. Stakeholders should begin now to address the benefits and costs of such a pipeline and the regulatory approvals that would be involved in such a decision. However, if the ban were lifted, the economic case for building such a pipeline would dissipate, with attention shifted to exporting the crude through existing or possibly new pipelines to Gulf Coast export facilities.

In none of our scenarios for the electricity TS&D system did we find problems in building, at reasonable cost, the additional transmission that would be needed. However, even in these scenarios, current industry could satisfy demand for new transmission lines without difficulty. What would be challenging would be the need for improved grid operations to manage a much more decentralized and distributed generation system.

For natural gas, strong U.S. production growth and changing supply and demand patterns are likely to create a need for additional pipeline capacity and restructuring of natural gas flows, but, in all of the scenarios examined, the expected expansion is within historical norms and can be accommodated through normal natural gas–industry expansion.

We also looked at the resilience of the petroleum and refined-oil products and the electricity TS&D systems and identified disruptive events in which regional disruptions would be possible, but in no instance did we identify a plausible scenario that would lead to prolonged systemic outages of these networks at a national scale.

Acknowledgments

We would like to thank William F. Hederman, Jr., and Lara Pierpoint for their support, guidance, and engagement that have been crucial to the conduct of this analysis. Alex C. Breckel provided helpful comments on the chapter on electric power. We would also like to thank the many staff members of the Office of Energy Policy and Systems Analysis and other analysts in the U.S. Department of Energy for working with us to develop and run the various energy future cases that form the basis of our work. We were particularly grateful for the assistance from the National Renewable Energy Laboratory and its researchers Nathan Blair, Wesley Cole, Daniel Steinberg, and Patrick Sullivan for collaborating with us to conduct the analysis of the electric power sector.

Our RAND colleague Blair Smith provided excellent support in formatting and preparing the document.

Abbreviations

AEO2014	2014 Annual Energy Outlook
AFV	alternative-fuel vehicle
Bcfd	billions of cubic feet per day
CNG	compressed natural gas
CO_2	carbon dioxide
CSP	concentrating solar power
DPV	distributed photovoltaic
EIA	U.S. Energy Information Administration
EPA	U.S. Environmental Protection Agency
EPSA	Office of Energy Policy and Systems Analysis
EV	electric vehicle
GHG	greenhouse gas
GW	gigawatt
LDV	light-duty vehicle
LNG	liquefied natural gas
LP	linear programming
Mb/d	thousands of barrels per day
MMb/d	millions of barrels per day
MW-mile	megawatt-mile
NEMS	National Energy Modeling System
NERC	North American Electric Reliability Corporation
NGL	natural gas liquids
NREL	National Renewable Energy Laboratory

ORNL	Oak Ridge National Laboratory
PADD	Petroleum Administration for Defense District
PV	photovoltaic
QER	Quadrennial Energy Review
RDM	Robust Decision Making
ReEDS	Regional Energy Deployment System
SPR	Strategic Petroleum Reserve
Tcf	trillions of cubic feet
TES	thermal energy storage
TRIM	Total Risk Integrated Model
TS&D	transmission, storage, and distribution
VMT	vehicle-mile traveled
W	watt

CHAPTER ONE

Introduction

Purpose

The purpose of this analysis is to help the U.S. Department of Energy Office of Energy Policy and Systems Analysis (EPSA) assess how energy transmission, storage, and distribution (TS&D) systems will perform under high-stress scenarios in which major shifts in energy demand, supply, or other uncertain factors have the potential to dramatically change the U.S. energy system by 2030. RAND researchers developed an analytical framework and associated metrics for examining vulnerabilities, opportunities, and risks to U.S. energy systems through 2030 under a range of uncertainties. We assess major stresses on and opportunities in the three major TS&D systems: oil and refined products, electric power, and natural gas. This analysis was requested to support the 2015 Quadrennial Energy Review (QER). The QER, which focuses on energy TS&D systems in its first volume, is a federal government initiative to systematically examine energy system performance and explore options to improve that performance to address 21st-century objectives.

Approach

We began our analysis by first identifying a small set of practical metrics describing U.S. energy TS&D system performance and vulnerabilities. This analysis then took an empirical approach to developing scenarios that would stress the TS&D systems, in contrast to the more common approach of selecting a set of scenarios for analysis a priori. This approach is particularly useful when the probabilities of future uncertain events or key changes in TS&D systems cannot be easily quantified. For each system, we explore the effects of varying assumptions regarding future supply and demand that revealed long-term vulnerabilities and opportunities within each TS&D system through 2030 by drawing on several existing simulation models of the U.S. energy system. Finally, we consider, in qualitative terms, the resilience of TS&D systems under selected disruptive events.

Robust Decision Making

EPSA asked RAND to support the scenario-analysis component of the QER in part because of our development of and experience with Robust Decision Making (RDM). RDM is an analytical framework for developing policy-relevant scenarios that reveal vulnerabilities of any type of physical or operating system under a set of uncertainties whose precise nature cannot be described using probability distributions.[1] In its most thorough implementation, RDM is interactive and employed through a participatory decisionmaking process with stakeholders and decisionmakers. As illustrated in Figure 1.1, RDM typically involves an initial step of decision structuring: identifying a proposed initial strategy along with goals, metrics, policy levers, system relationships and models, and uncertainties. RDM also requires a mathematical model of the system of interest and a business-as-usual (or proposed new) strategy or set of operating rules that will guide how the system will function in the future. In a typical application, the system model is run hundreds or thousands of times to generate a wide range of possible future realizations of system performance (called *cases*), distinguished by varying uncertain factors across plausible ranges (but for which a technically defensible probability distribution does not exist). This is called *case generation*.

An exploratory analysis, when coupled with a scenario-discovery algorithm (a mathematical approach to finding clusters of cases in which vulnerabilities in a system are estimated to be highest) leads to the identification of policy-relevant scenarios. That is, in contrast to a more typical scenario analysis, in which scenarios are hand-crafted at the start of an analysis, RDM runs the analysis backward and seeks to identify policy-relevant scenarios as an outcome of the analysis: One does not begin with scenarios in RDM; rather, scenarios emerge from the exploratory analysis.[2] In contrast to a more traditional predict-then-act analytical approach, in which a system is simulated to predict the future and then tested for its sensitivity to a range of conditions, RDM begins with a system as it currently operates and examines many different cases to identify the combination of uncertain factors that stress the system and thus reveal its vul-

Figure 1.1
Conceptual Diagram of the Robust Decision Making Process

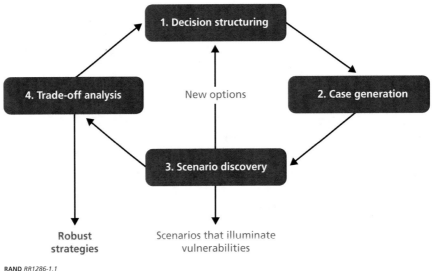

---

[1]   RAND Corporation, undated (b), lists numerous references that describe RDM in more detail. See also Lempert, Popper, and Bankes, 2003.

[2]   Scenario-discovery processes identify clusters of cases in the n-dimensional uncertainty space in which the system model projects some threshold level of vulnerability. The idea is to identify the conditions or levels of those uncertain factors that give rise to the clustering. These conditions then define a policy-relevant scenario. See "Futures Methodologies" (RAND Corporation, undated [a]) for more details.

nerabilities under current policies. *Vulnerabilities* are defined as specific levels of performance metrics, below or above which a system fails to meet performance expectations in some sense. Scenarios emerge from this kind of analysis by observing clusters of cases that exhibit system failure or vulnerability. The combinations of uncertain factors that give rise to these clusters are the scenarios of interest. When a full RDM analysis is conducted, examination of system performance under the high-stress scenarios leads to insights about new operating strategies, investments, policies, and other actions to mitigate those stresses.

In the absence of comprehensive system-modeling tools for U.S. energy TS&D infrastructure, we could not implement an RDM analysis in the time frame of this QER. However, we have employed the conceptual approach of RDM by working through a systematic process of identifying stressing scenarios for assessing vulnerabilities of the TS&D systems of interest to EPSA in response to a selected set of stresses. With limitations on model runs available to us within the time frame of the study, we truncated the generation of cases and instead moved more directly to identify scenarios of interest.

To illustrate the extent of resilience within the selected TS&D systems, we took a more qualitative approach to identifying short-duration, disruptive events. Not only is this analysis relevant for the current QER effort focused on energy TS&D systems; it can be extended as a foundational framework for future QER analysis on production and consumption, as well as other topics.

Steps Toward Creating Scenarios

1. Select Performance Metrics

We used a small number of selected metrics consistent with the QER goals of economic competitiveness, low environmental footprint, and energy security. We identify them in subsequent chapters in the context of each of the TS&D systems. We worked with EPSA to focus on a subset of performance metrics that are most feasible, given current modeling capabilities.

2. Choose System Models and Data

For consistency, we conducted all analyses of scenarios with models used elsewhere in the QER; we did not develop any of our own models for this study. References are provided in Appendix A. We collaborated with EPSA to draw on these existing system models to identify key vulnerabilities and opportunities associated with each system as reflected in the performance metrics. The base case for each of the TS&D systems was the Reference case from the 2014 Annual Energy Outlook (AEO2014) (U.S. Energy Information Administration [EIA], 2014a). For crude-oil and refined-oil products, we used the AEO2014 High Oil Output case, the Reference refined-oil product–consumption case, and our own RAND Low Consumption case for refined-oil products to develop additional scenarios. For the TS&D systems for electric power, we used model runs from the National Renewable Energy Laboratory's (NREL's) Regional Energy Deployment System (ReEDS) model to estimate effects on performance under various scenarios. For natural gas, we employed output of pipeline capacity and miles from the Deloitte MarketPoint World Gas model. We briefly describe model features in Appendix A.

3. Identify Key Uncertainties

For each system, we worked with EPSA to identify key uncertain factors bearing on production, consumption, and other factors that could affect the trajectory of a TS&D system's performance through 2030. These uncertain factors do not have probabilities associated with them.

4. Choose Policy Options

We examined the TS&D systems as they operate under current policy, as well as a limited set of potential future policies. For example, we examined the implications of ending the current ban on exports of U.S. domestically produced oil in our assessments of the oil and refined-oil product TS&D system. In the case of electricity, we evaluated the implications of steep, policy-driven reductions in emissions of greenhouse gases (GHGs).

5. Conduct the Vulnerability and Scenario Analysis

On our request, the developers of each of the models for each of the systems ran those models under varying assumptions of the key factors previously identified (detailed in Appendix A). Given time and modeling constraints for this QER, we necessarily needed to restrict model runs to a small number. In lieu of generating hundreds or thousands of cases, as we would in a fully implemented RDM analysis, we examined system performance against a base case over the time period of interest by considering one uncertain factor at a time to bound possible changes in system performance that might be associated with this factor alone. Where high or low values did not stress the system—on the evidence of an actual model run or, in its absence, by our own professional judgment—we noted those outcomes and eliminated those from further consideration. We designed the exercise to identify those factors in which changes in values assumed in the relevant base case had the greatest effect on the performance metrics of interest.

We also explored changes in combinations of multiple factors to identify key vulnerabilities and opportunities, selecting combinations by hand (versus a machine-generated scenario-discovery algorithm) based on the magnitude of effects associated with the particular uncertain factors. Because we had few model runs of individual cases with which to work, we could not implement a formal scenario-discovery process. In the case of both electricity and natural gas, we moved directly to identifying scenarios of interest from basic building blocks of cases previously run for AEO2014.

6. Discuss Resilience

Without use of mathematical models and the analysis of individual cases, we also identified disruptive events to the TS&D systems through the lens of resilience. We define *resilience* as the state of service from a system resulting in response to a disruption. Our focus here is on acute events (e.g., natural or human-caused disasters) and not slower-moving changes (e.g., climate change). In the absence of appropriate modeling tools, we instead used a qualitative approach to analyze resilience, which entails identifying where concerns about resilience might emerge and describing policy issues or questions that should be addressed.

Organization of This Report

In the following three chapters, we examine the vulnerabilities of petroleum and refined-oil products, electric power, and natural gas systems through 2030, following the approach outlined above. We then conclude by recapitulating our findings and assessing their significance for policymaking and long-term investments.

CHAPTER TWO

Petroleum and Refined-Oil Products

In the past several years, trends starting in the 1970s in U.S. crude-oil and refined-oil product markets have reversed: U.S. consumption of refined-oil products and natural gas liquids is down, while production has risen. As shown in Figure 2.1, in 2014, consumption had fallen to 8 percent below its peak in 2006, while U.S. crude-oil production had risen sharply (EIA, 2014c; EIA, 2014a). These two changes have driven and will likely continue to drive changes in petroleum and refined-oil product TS&D systems.

The reduction in demand for refined-oil products between 2006 and 2014 in absolute terms has been largely driven by changes in the transportation sector (EIA, 2014c; see, for example, Table 3.7c). Improved vehicle fuel efficiency has resulted in lower demand for gaso-

Figure 2.1
Historical and Projected U.S. Production of Crude Oil and Consumption of Petroleum and Other Liquids

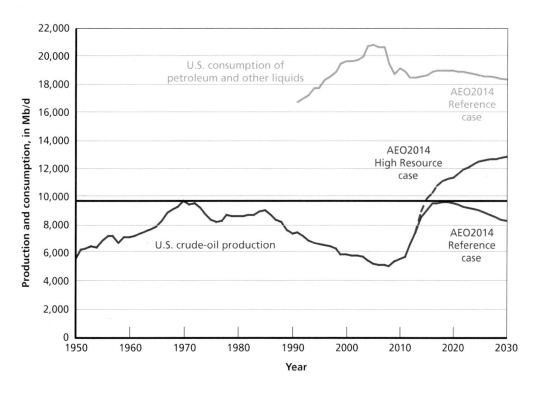

SOURCES: EIA, 2014a, 2014c.
NOTE: Mb/d = thousands of barrels per day.
RAND *RR1286-2.1*

line, as has reductions in per capita vehicle-miles traveled (VMT) stemming from the aging population and less interest in driving by teenagers and people in their 20s.[1] Another factor includes increasing availability and acceptance of alternative-fuel vehicles (AFVs), such as electric-powered cars and ethanol and flex-fuel vehicles (Federal Highway Administration, 2014).

Most of the new supply of crude oil comes from shale-oil plays in Texas and North Dakota; the latter is now producing at levels far beyond any seen before (North Dakota Industrial Commission, undated; Platts, 2013). These increases in quantity and shifts in location of supply are reshaping the means and destinations of oil transportation within the United States.

These changes in crude-oil flows are occurring in the context of two major constraints. Oil, unlike natural gas or electricity, can readily be transported via a variety of modes, including barge, rail, and truck, but the first and least expensive choice is generally pipeline. Pipeline construction is booming in the new oil-producing regions in North Dakota and Texas (Platts, 2013; Davies, 2013; Association of American Railroads, 2013). These new pipelines are bringing this oil directly to major hubs and refineries up and down the center of the country, including Cushing, Oklahoma, and Patoka, Illinois, but not to the East and West Coasts.

However, new pipeline construction has not kept pace with production: As a consequence of the lack of pipelines, 70 percent of the oil from the Williston and Bakken formations is being transported by rail, much of it to Philadelphia-area refineries designed for such crude. All of this oil being transported to refineries in California goes by rail and barge. As a result, a massive increase in rail transport has accompanied the production boom. Railroads have been stressed as a result (Frittelli et al., 2014; Steffy, 2014; RBN Energy, 2014). Increased volumes of oil hauled by railroad are slowing movement of other commodities, including coal from the Powder River Basin and wheat from North Dakota and Montana (González, 2014; Gilmour, 2014).

A second constraint on the movement of crude oil stems from the U.S. government's ban on exporting domestically produced crude except to Canada. According to IHS, an economic forecasting firm and consultancy, the export ban has reduced wellhead prices of domestic crude because of a mismatch between increased output of domestic tight light oil and the configuration of U.S. refining capacity (IHS, 2015). Gulf Coast refiners have invested heavily in complex processing facilities to process heavy, sour imported crude oils that are generally available at a discount to light sweet crude oil. According to EPSA analyses, in 2012, 67 percent of crude oil refined on the Gulf Coast was imported; 49 percent of these imports were heavy sour, and another 38 percent medium or light sour. Because of the ban on exports of crude oil, producers of light crude have had to offer their product at a discount to the international market price of Brent crude oil in order to move their product because such a large share of U.S. refining capacity is configured for heavier crudes. The lower price for tight light oil dampens upstream investment (IHS, 2015, p. 7).

Key Issues

Given the status of the crude-oil TS&D system in the United States and the ongoing changes in the quantity and distribution of production and consumption of refined-oil products, we

---

[1]   See McCahill, 2014, for a qualitative discussion of other drivers of VMT reductions.

have identified some questions of which policymakers need to be aware as they consider statutory, regulatory, and administrative actions that could affect private-sector investments in oil and refined-oil product TS&D systems.

First, between 2015 and 2030, are there scenarios under which parts of the TS&D system for crude-oil and refined-oil products will prove inadequate to meet the demands placed on them? If so, where and when are these shortfalls likely to occur, and what are the implications? Large shifts in the quantity and location of production and consumption of refined-oil products will, in the absence of corresponding changes in the TS&D system, have effects on the latter's reliability, affordability, sustainability, and safety. Policymakers need to understand where and to what extent there might be risks to these systems.

Second, where is new capacity likely to be needed? What form will (or should) that new capacity take (e.g., pipeline and rail)? What factors, be they economic, regulatory, or other, might inhibit needed capacity from being developed? Are state or federal actions contributing to those roadblocks, or, conversely, could any actions alleviate them?

A third set of questions centers on resiliency. To what extent is the TS&D system resilient to disruption? What new or improved capabilities might make the system more resilient, and what federal or state actions could contribute to this end? This part of the analysis will also focus on the East and West Coasts, where bottlenecks in the TS&D system present potential resiliency risks.

For this analysis, we define regions by the Petroleum Administration for Defense Districts (PADDs), as shown in Figure 2.2. Much of the analysis related to the first two sets of questions above focuses on how light crude oil from the new production centers in PADD 2 can be transported to the light crude–focused refiners on the East Coast, as well as other destinations. We

Figure 2.2
Petroleum Administration for Defense Districts

SOURCE: EIA, undated.

also explore the implications of removing the export ban and whether regional shifts in flows caused by reduced demand are likely to have significant effects on the TS&D system.

Performance Metrics

As the first step in our approach outlined in Chapter One, we focused on the following performance metrics to evaluate the performance of domestic TS&D systems for crude-oil and refined-oil products under different production, consumption, and policy conditions:

- reliability: the degree to which available transport and storage capacity can consistently manage interregional flows by volume from producing areas to consuming areas
- affordability: comparative costs of transporting oil per barrel per 1,000 miles by alternative mode between regions
- sustainability: comparative GHG emissions of transporting oil per barrel per 1,000 miles by alternative mode between regions
- transport safety: comparative numbers of barrels of oil spilled per 1,000 barrels per 1,000 miles by alternative mode between regions.

Models and Data

In our second step, we drew on EPSA analyses that used the AEO2014 Reference and High Resource oil-output cases and that employed the Ponderosa model and Oak Ridge National Laboratory (ORNL) Total Risk Integrated Model (TRIM) for their analyses and projections. We developed our own RAND Low Consumption case, described below and in Appendix B, to explore a wider range of stresses on the system.

Key Uncertainties

In the third step of our approach, we sought to identify the conditions that have the greatest potential to stress the TS&D systems across the performance metrics listed above. We therefore identified scenarios that capture different combinations of uncertain factors that are most likely to stress the capacity and reliability of TS&D systems for oil and refined-oil products according to those metrics. We worked with the EPSA team to identify plausible ranges for each of the uncertain factors. This effort indicated which of these factors, or combinations of factors, were likely to have the greatest impact on U.S. TS&D systems for oil and refined-oil products. The factors considered and the levels chosen for analysis are as follows:

- **crude-oil production:** Great uncertainty exists regarding the extent and longevity of the current shale-oil boom. The Reference case suggests that production will peak before 2020 and fall back below 2014 levels by 2030. By contrast, the AEO2014 High Oil and Gas Resource case (the High Resource case) projects much higher output of shale oil, such that domestic production of crude oil continues to increase, reaching a 2030 level that is 54 percent greater than in the Reference case (Figure 2.1). We use these two projections to bound oil output. Note that we did not select a Low Production case for analysis. Our objective was to identify cases that could stress the TS&D system; reduced production would alleviate rather than increase stress (less oil moving through pipelines requires less pipeline capacity).

- **refined-oil product demand:** We use the Reference case for demand, which shows an immediate increase that flattens out by around 2020, declining slightly after that year (Figure 2.1). No AEO2014 alternative case projects demand that varies greatly from that in the Reference case; in 2030, the lowest alternative projection is about 10 percent below the Reference case. However, demand for refined-oil products might well drop below those levels over the course of the next two decades because of changes in transportation demand. If adoption of AFVs accelerates (driven in part by the availability of inexpensive natural gas and improved battery technology), fuel economy continues to rise, or current downward trends in VMT continue, the United States could experience far greater reductions in refined-oil product use than in any of the AEO2014 projections. If consumption falls, flows of refined-oil products will shift more toward export markets. For these reasons, we have constructed the RAND Low Consumption case. Reduced consumption might not greatly stress the TS&D system for refined-oil products, but the associated shifts in refined-oil product sources and destinations could strain the current system.

Policy Options

The fourth step of the approach is to identify policy options. When building scenarios from the crude-oil production cases, we considered two alternatives: (1) continuation and (2) cessation of the export ban. This policy change would affect to where and potentially how crude oil flows. Another potential policy change relating to reductions in GHG emissions would be subsumed in the RAND Low Consumption case. In the context of resilience, we consider, in qualitative terms, what would happen if all rail shipments of crude oil were shut down following a major spill.

Scenario Analysis

EPSA identified four building-block cases for constructing scenarios of interest. These included the following:

- Reference case production (AEO2014)
- Reference case consumption (AEO2014)
- High Resource case production (AEO2014)
- RAND Low Consumption case (RAND, described below).

The Reference production, Reference consumption, and High Resource cases are from AEO2014, where they are well documented. The trajectories of output under these two cases are shown in Figure 2.1. However, we concluded that AEO2014's alternative cases for consumption could, in fact, be pushed down further. We therefore developed our own RAND Low Consumption case.

Description of the RAND Low Consumption Case

We began with the AEO2014 Reference case consumption of petroleum and other liquids, as shown in Figure 2.1. These projections are largely driven by transportation consumption, which accounted for 73 percent of total consumption in 2012. After transportation, the industrial sector accounted for the next-largest share of consumption. However, much of industrial use was for petrochemical and other manufacturing processes rather than for fuel. In constructing our RAND Low Consumption case, we leave industrial, residential, and commercial use unchanged from their levels in the Reference case and focus on potential changes in transportation use. Within transportation, we adopt the Reference case projections for jet fuel and fuel for other uses (e.g., recreational boating) and focus only on road, rail, and shipping in our analysis. Appendix B details our assumptions and analysis for consumption by these sectors within the RAND Low Consumption case. Figure 2.3 shows the Reference case and the RAND Low Consumption case.

Reference case consumption data are also available on a regional basis, but these regions do not exactly map to the PADDs. We estimate consumption by PADD by combining the regional projections with projections of U.S. population growth by state (U.S. Census Bureau, 2012, 2013). Although overall consumption is relatively flat for the time period in question, demographic shifts drive increases in consumption of refined-oil products in PADD 3 and reductions in PADDs 1 and 2. For our RAND Low Consumption case, we project the regional distribution of consumption to match the Reference case projections. AFVs will likely achieve much greater penetration in certain regions—notably, PADD 5—than others; further refine-

Figure 2.3
U.S. Consumption of Petroleum and Other Liquids

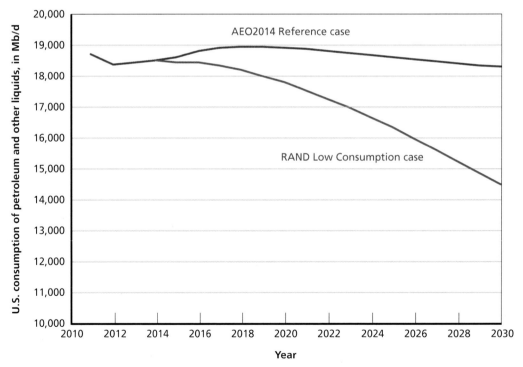

SOURCE: EIA, 2014a.

RAND RR1286-2.3

ment of this model could take that into account. We do not have regional data by transportation mode from the AEO2014 projections; we assume that international shipping is distributed between PADDs 1, 3, and 5 and domestic shipping between PADDs 2 and 3. The distribution of consumption by PADD in 2030 is shown in Figure 2.4 for both the Reference case and the RAND Low Consumption case. By 2030, overall consumption in the RAND Low Consumption case is 20 percent lower than in the Reference case.

Scenario Development

Building on these individual cases, EPSA constructed the first four scenarios for analysis summarized in Table 2.1. We then developed our own scenario based on very low consumption of refined-oil products. Each of these scenarios represents a combination of uncertain factors and further assumes either the continuation or elimination of the export ban.

Figure 2.4
Consumption of Petroleum and Other Liquids, 2030, by Petroleum Administration for Defense District

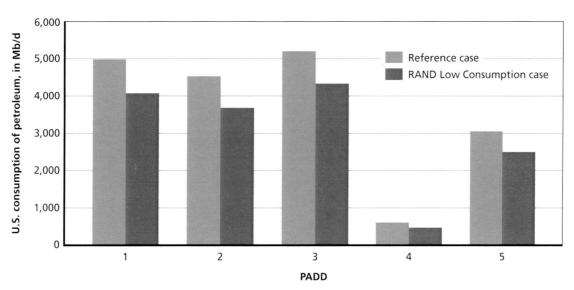

SOURCE: EIA, 2014a.
RAND RR1286-2.4

Table 2.1
Scenarios for Analysis

Scenario	Production Case	Consumption Case	Export Ban
1	Reference	Reference	In place
2	High Resource	Reference	In place
3	Reference	Reference	Lifted
4	High Resource	Reference	Lifted
5	Reference	RAND Low Consumption	In place

Reliability

EPSA conducted separate analyses of the ability to move crude oil under the first four scenarios. We conducted our own analysis for the fifth scenario. As noted above, most of the increased output of U.S. crude oil has come from the Williston Basin (Bakken) in North Dakota and Montana and the Eagle Ford and Permian basins in Texas. EPSA found that pipeline companies have responded to the new oil-transport demands primarily with extensive modifications of existing pipelines, including reversing the direction of flows and repurposing natural gas pipelines for oil, and by constructing a limited number of new pipelines.

Despite these efforts to repurpose or build additional pipelines from the Eagle Ford and Permian basins to Houston, Corpus Christi, and other ports on the Texas coast and from North Dakota to such destinations as Cushing, Oklahoma, and Patoka, Illinois, rail and barge continue to play a major role in moving tight oil to U.S. refineries, especially from the Bakken to the East and West Coasts. See Figure 2.5.

EPSA concluded that, under scenario 1, currently proposed commercial pipeline projects—together with rail loading and off-loading facilities—will provide sufficient capacity to transport increased domestic crude-oil production projected to 2030. Additional pipeline capacity plays an important role in ensuring that this oil can be moved. In fact, EPSA concluded that, without additional pipeline capacity, especially the conversion of Canada's Energy East Pipeline from natural gas to crude oil, an estimated 600,000 barrels per day of Western Canadian crude could be shut in prior to 2030.

Figure 2.5
Major Crude Rail Routes from Petroleum Administration for Defense District 2 West to the East Coast, Gulf Coast, and West Coast

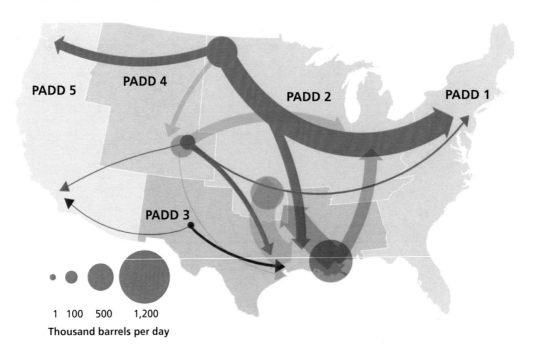

SOURCE: Farber-DeAnda, 2015, p. 9.
NOTE: Inter-PADD pipeline flows are faded to highlight rail movements. Representational inter-PADD pipeline flows exclude short-distance movements.
RAND RR1286-2.5

In addition, failure to expand rail capacity would create challenges for producers in Alberta, Canada. Canadian oil shipped south to the United States by rail will continue to be substantial, even with the addition of Keystone XL and the Alberta Clipper expansion. EPSA analyses find that, in the event of delayed or canceled pipeline build-out in Canada (e.g., no Keystone XL and no Energy East), Western Canadian crude railed to the United States would be constrained. If no new rail capacity or pipeline is built, the lack of rail capacity in that scenario would result in the shut-in of some 600,000 barrels per day of Western Canadian crude.

There are concerns about U.S. railroad capacity as well. Congestion and delays on railroads in North Dakota and the Upper Midwest are already serious problems because oil competes with the industrial and agricultural sectors for rail capacity. The Congressional Research Service writes that

> BNSF (the railroad most directly serving the Bakken region) noted that its car loadings in North Dakota had more than doubled from 2009 to 2013, and that in October 2013, crude oil and agricultural car loadings surged by more than it could manage. Past experience has shown that railroad bottlenecks are not quickly resolved. (Frittelli et al., 2014, p. 17)

In scenario 2, additional demand for U.S. rail capacity would exacerbate the current situation, especially for crude being transported east to refineries in Pennsylvania, New Jersey, and Delaware. Although the volumes shipped by rail from the Bakken to Washington State and from there to California by barge in scenario 2 could lead to congestion, the potential stresses on railroads to transport crude oil are not nearly as great as to the East Coast.

In scenario 2, the configuration of U.S. refiners and limitations on railroad capacity might work to constrain U.S. production, which, in turn, would affect transportation demand. In this scenario, EPSA found potential constraints on domestic U.S. production because of the configuration of the U.S. refining sector. According to the Ponderosa model, the U.S. refining sector can handle up to about 12 millions of barrels per day (MMb/d) of U.S. production, depending on whether most production over 9 MMb/d has the preferred relative density (American Petroleum Institute gravity) of above 35 degrees. To meet this target, in addition to the availability of tight light crude, Canadian heavy-oil production would have to grow steadily and be available to U.S. refiners. However, when U.S. production exceeds 12 MMb/d, EPSA finds, the U.S. market becomes so saturated with light crude oil and condensates that refiners prefer to import heavier, costlier crudes from abroad rather than run additional, heavily discounted domestic crudes so as to preserve their yields. At that point, heavier crude oils give refiners a higher return than running additional cheap light crude. In scenario 2, the value of some domestic crude oils drops below the break-even price, and production would not be economical, limiting increases in oil production and therefore demand for transportation services.

In terms of transportation capacity, through 2025, EPSA concluded, under scenario 2, currently proposed commercial pipeline projects coupled with rail will provide sufficient capacity to transport the increased production of domestic crude oil to refineries. However, starting in 2025, under this scenario, some Gulf Coast crude oil could become economically infeasible to produce under assumed break-even prices because the ban on exports of crude oil pushes down prices of tight light domestic crude oil.

The elimination of the ban on U.S. exports of crude oil in scenarios 3 and 4 affect flows within the domestic infrastructure. Under the assumptions in scenario 4, ORNL TRIM finds that, by 2020, roughly 0.8 MMb/d of crude exports become economically feasible, according to EPSA. This number rises to 1 MMb/d in 2025 but declines thereafter. Under scenarios 3 and 4, Gulf Coast refiners stop importing light to medium crudes from abroad but continue to import heavy crude oil for refineries with specialized heavy crude processing capabilities. The Ponderosa model generates large export volumes. According to EPSA, it projects exports of 1.5 MMb/d within the next several years, rising to more than 2 MMb/d by 2025, and declining slightly thereafter. Under scenarios 3 and 4, most of the oil for export would come from the Eagle Ford and Permian formations, while Gulf Coast refiners would absorb Bakken crude in lieu of the exported crude from Texas formations. Additional pipelines would transport crude from the Texas formations. Crude from the Bakken would be transported by additional pipeline capacity, railroad, and barge to the Gulf Coast.

However, scenarios 3 and 4 would alleviate pressure on the U.S. railroad system. In scenario 3, the volume of Bakken crude oil hauled by rail could drop sharply by 2030 because additional pipeline capacity would be constructed to move crude oil from the Bakken south to ports along the Gulf of Mexico rather than east and west. However, in scenario 4, two additional pipelines are projected to be built that are not built in scenario 2.

In scenario 5, using the RAND Low Consumption case, demand drops by 20 percent from current levels, reaching about 14.4 MMb/d in 2030. Were such a scenario to play out, the movement of refined-oil products would have to shift to compensate for the declines in demand. For example, refineries in PADD 2 produce 5.0 MMb/d of petroleum products and other liquids per year, which is roughly balanced by annual consumption in this PADD of 4.8 MMb/d. By 2030, however, in this scenario with the RAND Low Consumption assumptions, PADD 2 refining capacity (assumed to be roughly unchanged) will significantly exceed demand, which drops to 3.6 MMb/d. Thus, Midwestern refiners would need to expand their service areas, displacing some product currently provided by coastal refiners or export product abroad. The same situation would occur in PADD 5, where demand (3.1 MMb/d) now roughly matches production (3.0 MMb/d). By 2030, the situation would flip, with supply exceeding demand by more than 20 percent. This extra coastal production could also serve a larger area or could be exported. Similarly, in PADD 1, where refining today meets about 67 percent of demand for products, that number would top 90 percent by 2030 in this RAND Low Consumption case. The Northeast and Mid-Atlantic regions, which currently receive product via the Colonial and Buckeye pipelines from PADD 3 or import product from abroad, would be able to satisfy their own demand.[2] However, we consider it unlikely that these changes in demand would greatly disrupt the TS&D system, particularly because they would develop gradually.

Under all scenarios, when all of the envisioned pipeline expansions are completed, rail-to-barge flows will decrease significantly.

Affordability

Table 2.2 shows projections by EPSA and IHS of new pipeline capacity that might be constructed through 2030 and its costs. Note that IHS projects substantially more pipeline construction than does EPSA.

In general, pipeline is preferable to rail for transporting crude oil because of cost. EPSA has found that the cost of transporting crude by rail runs $15 per barrel from the Bakken to the East Coast, $12 per barrel to the Gulf Coast, and $9 per barrel to the Northwest, contrasting

---

[2] Production numbers are from EIA, 2014c.

Table 2.2
Office of Energy Policy and Systems Analysis and IHS Projections Through 2030 of New Pipeline Capacity and Costs

Projection	EPSA		IHS	
	Capacity, in Mb/d	Capital Expenditures, in Billions of Dollars	Capacity, in Mb/d	Capital Expenditures, in Billions of Dollars
U.S.	11,960	34	17,939	52
Canada and Canada-U.S.	5,645	40	17,176	72
Total	17,605	74	35,115	124

SOURCES: Personal communications from EPSA and IHS staff to the authors.

with estimated costs of possibly $5 per barrel for transporting crude oil by pipeline. These rail costs are two to three times the cost of shipping by pipeline. These numbers are consistent with those of other analysts, who estimate that the cost of shipping by rail is $5 to $10 per barrel more than by pipeline (Davies, 2013; Frittelli et al., 2014).

Pipelines are expensive, however. The costs of the capital expenditures for building out the pipeline infrastructure shown in Table 2.2 would be $34 billion and $40 billion, respectively, for the U.S. and Canadian build-outs for the EPSA projections and $52 billion and $72 billion, respectively, for the IHS projections. Although these costs would be lumpy, spreading them evenly between 2014 and 2030 yields a range of investment expenditures of $2.1 billion to $3.3 billion per year for the United States and $2.5 billion to $4.8 billion per year for Canada. As reported by EPSA, in recent years, expenditures on crude-oil pipelines in the United States have been substantially more than these figures. IHS Global, 2013, found that expenditures on crude-oil pipelines in 2013 ran $6.6 billion, up from $1.6 billion in 2010.

The proposed pipelines should be profitable. The Sandpiper pipeline, which will run a total of 612 miles from North Dakota to Minnesota and carry 225,000 barrels per day in one segment and 375,000 barrels per day in a different segment, is estimated to cost $2.6 billion (Enbridge, undated). If operated at an assumed capacity of 225,000 barrels per day, the project could generate $1.1 million, $2.2 million, or $3.4 million per day based on charges of $5, $10, or $15 per barrel, respectively, for an estimated payback period for the investment of as little as two to six years. Savings over rail transportation could run $1.1 million to $2.2 million per day.

However, such new pipeline projects need to secure long-term commitments from shippers in order to obtain financing. In contrast, rail projects require only short-term contracts and offer more flexibility in moving oil to alternative markets when market conditions shift (Curtis et al., 2014). Consequently, despite the cost advantages, rail is expected to continue to play a much more important role in transporting crude oil than in the past, especially in a period of volatility in production volumes and prices.

According to EPSA analyses, only limited additional rail off-loading capacity is anticipated through 2030 for the United States even in scenarios 2 and 4. According to these analyses, the only significant potential bottleneck in the United States would be 400,000 barrels a day of off-loading capacity expansion planned for PADD 5 in 2015. If this project does not go through, the absence of this capacity could limit crude transport by rail from North Dakota, especially if planned pipelines are delayed or canceled.

The continued use of rail will need additional investments in railroads. According to IHS, projected investment by railroad to transport crude oil, natural gas liquids, and liquid petroleum gas between 2014 and 2025 would run $9.3 billion for crude oil and $6.7 billion to $7.5 billion for natural gas liquids and liquid petroleum gas. This yields total additional average annual investments in rail of roughly $1.5 billion.

Sustainability

We measure sustainability by the comparative GHG emissions of transporting oil per barrel per 1,000 miles by alternative modes between regions. However, assessment of mode-specific GHG emissions proved difficult to evaluate. Competing analyses have shown conflicting results as to relative GHG emissions associated with rail versus pipeline (Lemphers, 2013).

Transport Safety

Railroad safety is a growing concern. Some major accidents have involved crude oil transported by rail in recent years, including a derailment in Quebec that killed 47 people and several derailments that led to fires and explosions of oil-carrying cars. The U.S. federal government has approved new rules, including phasing out older tank cars in order to improve safety.

As shown in Figure 2.6, spillage has been generally lower in recent years when transporting oil by rail than by pipeline (trucks spill far more than either), but high-profile incidents have raised public concern about transport by rail (Frittelli et al., 2014).

Figure 2.6
Oil-Spill Volume per Billion Ton-Miles

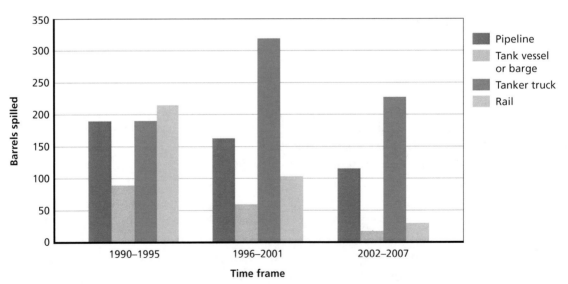

SOURCE: Frittelli et al., 2014, p. 11.
RAND *RR1286-2.6*

Resilience

We identified potential weak points in the existing infrastructure and drew on prior analysis and lessons from recent experience to discuss some of the potential associated challenges and solutions. We did not have the benefit of specific model runs to inform this discussion.

Despite reductions in consumption in recent years, refined-oil products play and will continue to play a major role in the U.S. economy. Americans depend on the availability of gasoline, heating oil, and other products. When the cost of these products rises rapidly, the U.S. economy and the lives of U.S. citizens can be disrupted.

In the past, disruptions to refined-oil product markets have come in two forms:

- global price shocks triggered by abrupt cutoffs in foreign supplies of oil or unexpected surges in global demand that suddenly drive up world market prices for oil
- regional or local supply disruptions and consequent price increases, usually triggered by natural disasters.

When natural disasters temporarily disrupt regional or local supplies or when global price shocks occur, there are costs to households and businesses. These costs can be particularly burdensome for lower-income households. However, in the context of longer-term stress on TS&D, these disruptions tend to be transient. In recent periods, the U.S. economy has become more resilient in the face of global oil price shocks than it was during the time of the 1973 oil embargo because Americans use gasoline and diesel more efficiently. The U.S. government created the Strategic Petroleum Reserve (SPR) to buffer the consequences of an abrupt disruption in global oil supplies. The SPR holds just under 700 million barrels of light crude oil (both sour and sweet) (U.S. Department of Energy, 2015b); crude oil can be withdrawn from the SPR at the maximum rate of 4.4 million barrels per day in response to a major disruption (Andrews and Pirog, 2012; U.S. Department of Energy, 2015a).[3]

The U.S. system of transporting and storing crude-oil and refined-oil products is generally robust and resilient in the face of disruptions. Oil and refined-oil products are shipped by a variety of modes: barge, pipeline, rail, and truck. When disruptions occur, shippers can shift cargoes across modes or, in the case of barge, rail, and road, add capacity by marshaling more ships and vehicles.

However, in the event of another major derailment that resulted in loss of life, government authorities could impose a moratorium on all rail shipments until safety procedures were reviewed and improved. If this moratorium were to last an extended period of time, months rather than weeks, some production from the Bakken would be shut in because currently other transportation modes would be unable to pick up the slack. Presumably, the effects would be transient as new safety procedures were adopted. If the moratorium were to be permanent, it would lead to a decline in output in the United States commensurate with the current amount of oil being transported by rail. Eventually, pipeline capacity could be expanded, but this would take some years.

---

[3] The U.S. Department of Energy claims a possible withdrawal rate of more than 4 MMb/d. See U.S. Department of Energy, undated. This number also appears in Andrews and Pirog, 2012. At the moment, the SPR holds 691 million barrels (U.S. Department of Energy, 2015b).

Experiences with refined-oil product supply following Hurricane Sandy highlight some weaknesses in distribution systems in the Mid-Atlantic states. Demand in the area is primarily served by the New York metropolitan area shipping terminals, New Jersey and Philadelphia-area refineries, and the Colonial and Buckeye pipeline terminals in Linden, New Jersey. Operations of all of these facilities were disrupted during and following Sandy—some from storm damage, but most from extended power outages. Many filling stations were unable to obtain fuel. Many of those that did were without electric power to operate their pumps: The resulting inability to obtain gasoline or diesel slowed relief and repair efforts (Center on Global Energy Policy, 2014; City of New York, 2013, pp. 136–142).

During Sandy, the Jones Act (formally, the Merchant Marine Act of 1920, Pub. L. 66-261) was waived, which facilitated barge delivery of refined-oil products from the Gulf Coast (U.S. Department of Homeland Security, 2012). However, other regulations, such as New York's laws restricting margins on deliveries of gasoline and diesel (to prevent price gouging), were not relaxed, which curtailed suppliers' ability to truck in fuel from other regions (City of New York, 2013, pp. 136–142). New York State has put forward one proposal to develop a predefined package of regulatory actions that can be taken immediately in response to an emergency, rather than figuring out appropriate steps after the event has occurred (Center on Global Energy Policy, 2014; City of New York, 2013, pp. 136–142).

Hardening distribution and delivery systems against extended power outages is another approach to improving resilience. There is a potential federal role in promoting such improvements, from implementing measures to increase the resilience of the electric power grid to providing incentives to set up backup power for pipelines, terminals, and filling stations. Facility operators often cannot justify the cost of backup power when disruptions are infrequent. For a region as a whole, however, the lack of distributed backup power could slow down the recovery and reconstitution process.

A third takeaway from Sandy was the need for appropriately sited refined-oil product reserves. Because of the long supply chain to the Mid-Atlantic states and the Northeast, the potential for such a large part of the chain to be disrupted by a single event, and the region's reliance on heating oil, extended disruptions of fuel-distribution systems could have serious consequences for vulnerable residents. In the aftermath of Sandy, the Department of Energy established the Northeast Home Heating Oil Reserve and the Northeast Regional Refined Petroleum Product Reserve, each of which holds 1 million barrels of product. Its cost-effectiveness in practice has not as yet been demonstrated. However, a systematic evaluation to identify similarly vulnerable regions and the need for such reserves could help improve resilience to major disruptions throughout the United States (Center on Global Energy Policy, 2014; City of New York, 2013, pp. 136–142).

Refined-oil product–distribution systems along the West Coast are more isolated from the rest of the country than other regions are. Refineries in the San Francisco Bay Area, the Los Angeles area, and the Central Valley meet most demand in the West. These refineries are located in earthquake zones. If, for example, a major earthquake were to severely damage the Los Angeles refineries, 500 Mb/d of capacity, one-third of the gasoline, diesel, and other refined products consumed west of the Rockies, would be off-line until the refineries could be repaired or, in the worst case, rebuilt (Ortiz, Samaras, and Molina-Perez, 2013). Replacing this supply would present major challenges, particularly in the face of damage to the Los Angeles ports themselves. The same holds if a terrorist attack were to severely damage refineries and import terminals in California; supplies would flow relatively soon after the event, albeit at a cost in terms of higher prices at the pump (Meade and Molander, 2006).

Replacing such a large quantity of refined-oil products would be difficult, but the current U.S. refined-oil product–distribution system should be adaptable enough to meet demand in southern California in such an event, just at additional cost. Part of the demand could be met by importing refined oil products through the Bay Area ports and then transporting by rail or truck to southern California. However, this would necessitate obtaining a waiver concerning the use of specially formulated gasoline and diesel, which is possible under the Energy Policy Act of 2005 (Pub. L. 109-58).[4] Existing product pipelines from the southern California refineries to northern California could be reversed. A combination of these three measures should be sufficient to cover almost all demand in southern California. These measures would push up the price of gasoline and diesel sharply, at least in the first several months.

Key Findings

- Recent increases in crude-oil output from the Bakken-Williston and Eagle Ford shales have put pressure on the U.S. TS&D system for crude oil, especially railroads moving crude oil out of the Bakken area to the East Coast.
- Under most scenarios, currently planned additions to pipeline capacity, coupled with existing use of rail, should be sufficient to handle projected increases in output. However, in the High Resource case with a continued ban on exports, a combination of lack of demand for tight light crude and constraints on railroad capacity could lead to shutting in some production.
- In the event that the ban on U.S. exports of crude oil is lifted, transportation patterns would shift. Crude oil from the Eagle Ford and Permian basins in Texas would likely be exported; crude from the Williston Basin in North Dakota would be shipped south to refineries on the Gulf of Mexico in lieu of tight light oil from Texas. Current transport of this crude by rail to the East Coast would fall.
- The very large cost differentials between hauling crude of rail versus pipeline (two or three times) will lead to continued expansion in crude-oil pipeline capacity. However, differences in projections of future capacity are large, with the highest projected increase in capacity for the United States running 50 percent more than the alternative.
- Large-scale use of rail to transport crude oil is likely here to stay because of the flexibility that rail provides.
- Competing analyses of GHG emissions associated with rail versus pipeline come up with different results.
- Spillage is generally lower when transporting oil by rail than by pipeline, but several high-profile incidents have raised public concern about transport by rail.
- In the event of another major derailment, especially one involving loss of life, government authorities could impose a moratorium on all rail shipments until safety procedures were

---

[4] The Energy Policy Act of 2005

includes provisions that will limit the future growth of new boutique fuels allowable under [Clean Air Act] Section 211(c) and provides additional authority to EPA [the U.S. Environmental Protection Agency] to waive boutique fuel requirements when necessary to help alleviate unexpected supply disruptions. (EPA, 2006, p. 3)

reviewed and improved. As long as such a moratorium is in place, it would severely affect production in the Bakken.

Electric Power

Since the beginning of the Great Recession, demand for electricity has fallen or stagnated, as shown in Figure 3.1. According to the AEO2014 Reference case, between 2013 and 2030, demand is projected to increase 17.4 percent, an average annual rate of 0.9 percent. Compared with those in past decades, this rate of increase is modest, but, compared with the past few years of stagnating demand, this forecast might even be high. Sources of supply are shifting as substantial amounts of older coal-fired capacity are being retired and policies are enacted requiring increased use of renewable resources. Electricity that these plants had generated is now being generated by natural gas–fired power plants and from wind energy. These shifts, especially toward wind energy, have placed new demands on the transmission grid. In the future, broader use of distributed generation, such as rooftop solar or smaller natural gas–powered generation for microgrids, could create new challenges for electricity transmission and distribution systems. The challenges of intermittency from wind and solar will also lead

Figure 3.1
Historical and Projected U.S. Consumption of Electricity, 2011–2030

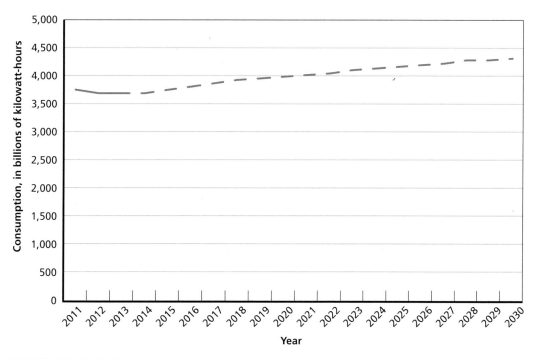

SOURCE: EIA, 2014a, Reference case.
RAND *RR1286-3.1*

to greater demand for electric storage. The California Public Utilities Commission is already mandating that electric power providers build storage capacity to ensure electric power can be reliably provided as intermittent sources of supply account for an increasing share of the generating mix (California Public Utilities Commission, 2013).

This chapter assesses projected impacts that a broad range of factors, including prospective change in sources of generation and electric power demand, could have on transmission capacity, energy prices, and GHG emissions. We also examined challenges in the context of TS&D systems' resilience to a variety of disruptions.

Key Issues

Continuing to satisfy demand for electric power in the face of potential capacity retirements in a manner that ensures affordable, reliable power in an environmentally sound manner is the key challenge facing the electric power TS&D system. Substantial amounts of U.S. coal-fired electric power–generating capacity could well be retired through 2030, under revised U.S. regulations limiting emissions from coal-fired power plants. Figure 3.2 shows EIA's projections of coal capacity retirements through 2040 from AEO2014. AEO2014 projects around 60 gigawatts (GW) of coal plant retirements by 2020, 20 percent of total coal-fired capacity, and 5 percent of total U.S. generation capacity. New regulations, including EPA's Mercury and Air Toxics Standards and Clean Power Plan rules, could lead to substantially higher retirements than EIA has projected.[1] Large amounts of nuclear capacity could be retired and replaced with other generation sources, as a consequence of high costs of new plant construction, costs of upgrades to extend licenses for aging plants, and competition from cheaper gas-fired generators. Replacing existing coal generating capacity to meet environmental constraints and

Figure 3.2
Projected Cumulative Retirements of Coal-Fired Generating Capacity, 2012–2040

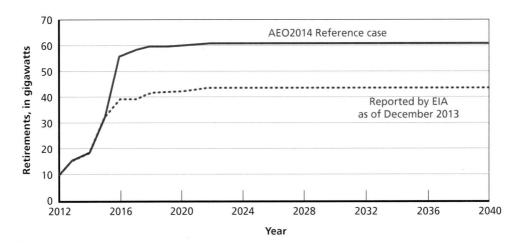

SOURCES: EIA, 2014a, Reference case; EIA, 2013c.
RAND RR1286-3.2

---

[1] EIA projections are based only on existing laws and not proposed regulations.

installing additional capacity as electric power demand grows could put stress on the TS&D system in some places where the location of generating capacity will have shifted.

In a future in which the U.S. government seeks to substantially reduce emissions of GHGs, on the order of 40 percent, major increases in generation from renewable energy sources, as well as natural gas, would be necessary. Wind power might require significant new transmission capacity, depending on where wind capacity is sited relative to electricity demand centers. Intermittent renewable technologies could drive increased demand for energy storage capacity. However, if future demand for electricity stagnates or even drops as a consequence of efficiency gains, or if the U.S. government puts less emphasis on reducing GHG emissions, existing coal plants with possibly some new additions near current sites and existing or new natural gas generation could serve to supply U.S. electricity demand without requiring major changes in TS&D systems within the bounds of the parameters explored.

Performance Metrics

To evaluate potential stresses on and opportunities for the U.S. electricity TS&D system under different production, consumption, and policy conditions posed by these prospective changes, we use the following performance metrics:

- transmission: demand for new transmission in megawatt-miles (MW-miles)[2]
- affordability: changes in retail electric power prices by region stemming from changes in generation and costs of expanding the transmission system
- sustainability: comparative GHG emissions under various futures.

Model and Data

We ran all scenarios through NREL's ReEDS model (Short et al., 2011). The major outputs of ReEDS include, by region, "the amount of generator capacity and annual generation from each technology, storage capacity expansion, transmission capacity expansion, total electric sector costs, electricity price, fuel prices, and carbon dioxide (CO_2) emissions" (NREL, 2015).

Key Uncertainties

We worked with EPSA to create a series of ten scenarios[3] of changes in power-generating technologies and capacity and shifts in demand for power within the United States through 2030 to evaluate potential stresses on the electric power TS&D system. We sought to vary individual factors and then combinations of factors that represent a range of stress scenarios for the U.S.

---

[2] A MW-mile is a unit of measure in transmission line capacity that represents a transmission line rated with a carrying capacity of 1 megawatt of power and a 1-mile extent.

[3] To simplify our discussion in this chapter, we refer to the variation of both single factors and combinations of factors as *scenarios* rather than distinguishing the single-factor variations as *cases* as done in Chapter Two.

electricity system through 2030.[4] The scenarios are shown in Table 3.1 and described in the following section. We further note that the selection of these scenarios does not imply their likelihood but rather reflects our informed judgment about the likely factors that could lead to higher-stress cases over the next 25 years.

We chose this set of ten scenarios because they provide an opportunity to assess vulnerabilities in the electric power system relative to the base case. The single-factor scenarios allow us to examine the consequences of individual, controlled changes in the energy model that affect outcomes of interest when compared to the base case. The combination scenarios show how multiple changes in the energy system can either exacerbate or mitigate the individual factor effects. Except where we note deviations from the base case, each scenario uses the baseline parameters (e.g., base-case demand).

Where we disaggregate our analysis by region, we report results for the NREL ReEDS regions that were defined in the Renewable Electricity Futures Study (NREL, 2012). ReEDS divides the United States into 356 resource-supply regions based in great part on the availabil-

Table 3.1
Scenarios Generated from Regional Energy Deployment System Model Runs

Scenario Type	Name	Summary Description
Base case	Base case	All baseline parameters (see Table 3.2)
Single factor	Low Wind Cost	Wind Vision high cost reduction (U.S. Department of Energy, 2015c)
Single factor	Low Solar Cost	Solar technologies achieve $1.50-per-watt (W) equivalent in 2020 and $1/W equivalent in 2040 (U.S. Department of Energy, 2012)
Single factor	High Natural Gas Prices	AEO2014 Low Oil and Gas Resource
Single factor	High Distributed Photovoltaics	SunShot Vision price declines of 62.5 to 75 percent
Single factor	Low Demand	AEO2014 Low Electricity Demand
Single factor	High Demand	AEO2014 High Economic Growth
Combination	Greenhouse-Gas Emission Cap + Reduced Demand	GHG cap; reduced demand
Combination	Greenhouse-Gas Emission Cap + High Nuclear Retirements + High Natural Gas Prices	GHG cap, high nuclear retirements, high natural gas prices
Combination	Greenhouse-Gas Emission Cap + High Renewable-Energy Penetration[a] + Reduced Demand	GHG cap, low wind cost, low solar cost, reduced demand,[b] high PV, low storage cost
Combination	High Renewable-Energy Penetration + Reduced Demand	Low wind cost, low solar cost, reduced demand,[b] high PV, low storage cost

SOURCE: Cases created by EPSA, RAND, and NREL.

NOTE: PV = photovoltaic.

[a] High Renewable-Energy Penetration = low wind cost, low solar cost, high PV penetration, and low storage cost.

[b] The QER Reduced Electricity Demand case is a special demand case designed to accompany the Low GHG case in most model runs. It is similar to the AEO2014 Low Electricity Demand case, with slightly higher levels of energy use across all years.

[4]   To capture stresses that could affect the TS&D system around 2030, we ran these cases through 2050 as well.

ity of renewable energy resources within each region. These regions are then aggregated into balancing areas, areas that are or might be connected by transmission lines to balance demand with available supplies of renewable energy, reserve-sharing groups, and finally a close approximation to North American Electric Reliability Corporation (NERC) regions (NREL, 2014). For the purposes of this analysis, we focus on the NERC regions: (1) Northwest, (2) Great Plains, (3) Great Lakes, (4) Northeast, (5) Mid-Atlantic, (6) Southeast, (7) Central, (8) Texas, (9) Southwest, (10) California, and (11) Florida. We provide a map of these NERC regions in Figure 3.3.

Base Case

The QER's base case serves as a common point of departure for all of the scenarios we explored in the analysis. The base case is based on the AEO2014 Reference case. However, some key parameter assumptions embedded in the ReEDS model differ from those in AEO2014.[5]

Table 3.2 summarizes the assumptions embedded in the QER's base case that are relevant to our analysis. For the RAND analysis, we seek to demonstrate, through our selection of scenarios, how these assumptions might affect system performance. We did not, however, explore the validity of each of these assumptions.

We derived the base case's assumptions regarding regional variations in power plant cost from a 2013 study that estimated such variations by accounting for regional differences in climate, seismic design, remoteness, urban high-density population issues, labor wage and productivity differences, and projected increases in overhead associated with location (EIA, 2013a, p. 2-5).

In this section, we discuss the six building-block scenarios built from the base case that were represented in the ReEDS model runs.

Low Wind Cost Scenario

Wind power assumptions in the Low Wind Cost scenario are informed by the Department of Energy's Wind Vision study (U.S. Department of Energy, 2015c). Wind Vision represents a variety of "aggressive but attainable" growth scenarios for the wind energy industry, revisiting the claims of a 2008 department report titled *20% Wind Energy by 2030* (U.S. Department of Energy, 2008). For this scenario, we assume that land-based wind overnight capital costs fall from $1,590 to $1,782 per kilowatt in 2013 to $1,281 to $1,540 per kilowatt in 2030.[6]

---

[5] The National Energy Modeling System (NEMS) and ReEDS are structured very differently: Even given the exact same inputs, they will give different answers. For example, ReEDS has 134 regions to NEMS's 18. ReEDS considers only the electricity sector, while NEMS considers all energy sectors and the interplays between them. ReEDS does not represent self-consumed electricity (e.g., behind-the-fence combined heat and power), while NEMS does. ReEDS handles renewable-energy capacity value and curtailment calculations much differently from how NEMS handles them. ReEDS represents wind and solar resources with more granularity than NEMS does, which changes how much and where things get deployed. ReEDS represents transmission and transmission constraints, which changes where and how much generation gets built. NEMS has a representation of natural gas supply, while ReEDS uses static supply curves.

[6] The lower bounds are for generation when wind speeds are high, and the upper bound for when wind speeds are low. The figures are in 2013 dollars, which are a little less than 2 percent more than 2012 dollars, the unit used elsewhere in the report.

Figure 3.3
North American Electric Reliability Corporation Region Map

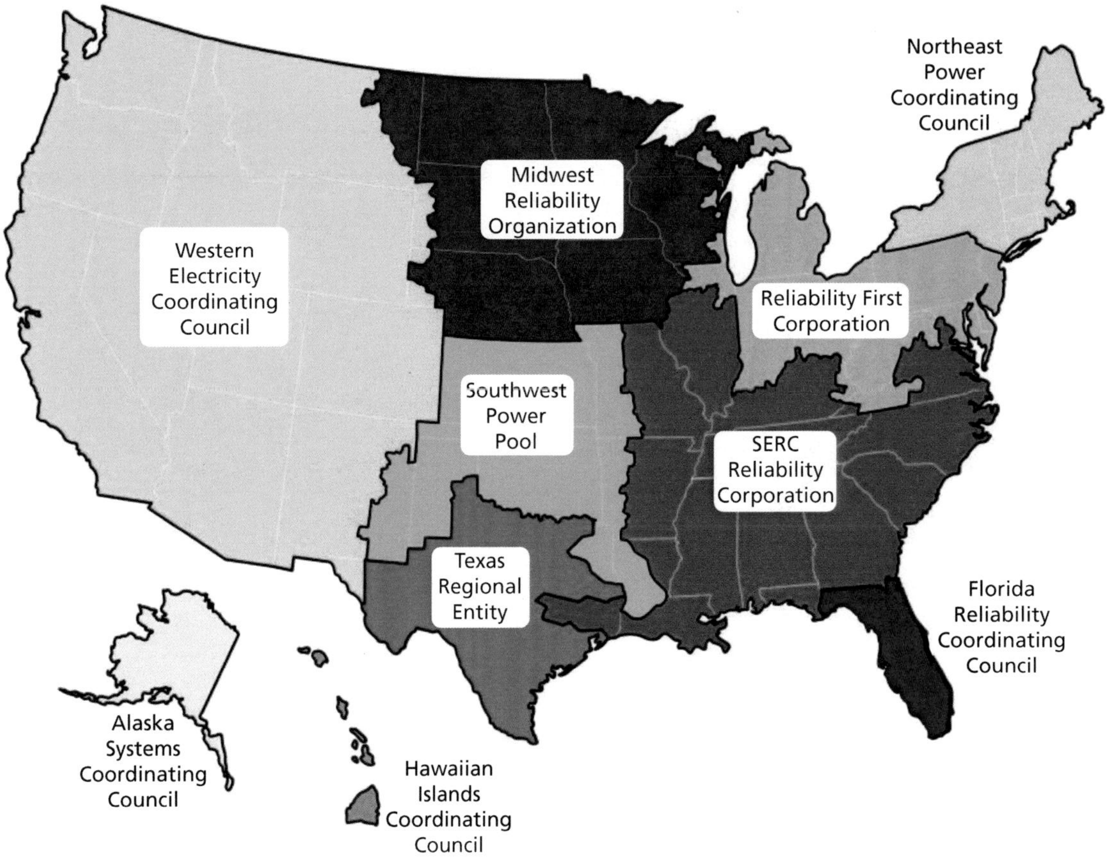

SOURCE: EPA, 2015.
NOTE: This is a representational map. Many of the boundaries shown are approximate because they are based on companies, not strictly geographic boundaries.
RAND RR1286-3.3

Low Solar Cost Scenario

The QER's Low Solar Cost scenario draws on the Department of Energy's 2012 SunShot Vision Study for parameter estimates regarding utility-level PV, distributed PV (DPV), and concentrating solar power (CSP) with thermal energy storage (TES). In particular, the Low Solar Cost scenario refers to a scenario from the SunShot Vision Study in which prices for utility-level PV, DPV, and CSP with TES are assumed to fall by 62.5 percent between 2010 and 2020 and achieve a 75-percent cost reduction in 2040. In most respects, solar assumptions would match those of the SunShot Vision Study's "SunShot" scenario (U.S. Department of Energy, 2012, p. 5).

The QER Low Solar Cost scenario also relies on a 2012 study by Black and Veatch for parameter estimates regarding CSP without TES. Key assumptions from the Black and Veatch study are listed in the report (Black and Veatch, 2012, p. 3).[7]

---

[7] All CSP power generation would be located in the Southwest United States; trough systems would be the technology of choice until 2025, after which tower systems would be constructed; CSP systems would be dry-cooled; and tower configurations would use multiple towers.

Table 3.2
Base-Case Outputs

Parameter	Based on	Values
Costs of conventional power generation, including coal, nuclear, conventional hydro, and natural gas (conventional and advanced combined cycle)	AEO2014 Reference case; hydro power capital costs are from Hall et al., 2003	See AEO2014
Solar costs (levelized cost of electricity), measured as CSP with storage, given in dollars per kilowatt	AEO2014 Reference case; alternatives from SunShot Vision Study	1,452 in 2010, 1,775 in 2030, and 1,775 in 2050
DPV costs, measured as installed capacity increases, given in gigawatts	AEO2014 Reference case; alternatives from SunShot Vision Study	1.8 in 2010, 33.6 in 2030, and 59.0 in 2050
Electricity demand (generation), given in terawatt-hours	AEO2014 Reference case[a, b]	3,936 in 2010, 4,507 in 2030, and 5,158 in 2050
Natural gas prices, given in 2010 dollars per million British thermal units	AEO2014 Reference case	5.02 in 2010, 6.15 in 2030, and 9.94 in 2050
Nuclear retirements	NREL assumes 60-year lifespan	99.4 GW total retirements between 2010 and 2050. Assumes nuclear plant life is 60 years.
Wind costs, given in dollars per kilowatt	AEO2014 Reference case	1,849 in 2010, 1,751 in 2030, and 1,710 in 2050

SOURCES: EIA, 2014a; Hall et al., 2003; U.S. Department of Energy, 2012; NREL, 2015.

[a] Initial 2010 demand is based on the 2010 Electric Power Annual (U.S. Department of Energy, 2011), which reported 2010 demand at 3,739 terawatt-hours. NREL adjusted this demand upward by 5.3 percent to account for distribution losses. Total demand does not include most self-served load and combined heat and power from Alaska and Hawaii.

[b] Demand in ReEDS is specified through region-specific growth parameters. Demand in each region-year is exogenously determined relative to the base year, 2010. We present total demand for simplification. ReEDS does not include industry-generated and consumed electricity but imputes a value based on AEO2014 demand projections.

High Natural Gas Prices Scenario

The High Natural Gas Prices scenario assumes that natural gas resource availability is lower than in the base case, resulting in higher natural gas prices. It is based on the Low Oil and Gas Resources scenario in AEO2014, in which the estimated ultimate recovery at shale wells is assumed to be 50 percent lower than in the AEO2014 Reference case (EIA, 2014a, p. IF-12). In this scenario, the average cost per million British thermal units of natural gas rises from $5.02 in 2010 (in 2010 dollars here and throughout this chapter) to $9.94 in 2050.

High Distributed Photovoltaics Scenario

The High Distributed Photovoltaics scenario (DPV stretch case) corresponds to a scenario analyzed in the Department of Energy's 2012 SunShot Vision Study. It assumes that prices for DPV power systems will fall by 62.5 percent between 2010 and 2020 and by a total of 75 percent by 2040, yielding 83 GW of DPV in 2030 and 245 GW of DPV in 2050 (U.S. Department of Energy, 2012, p. 263). This scenario is consistent with continued sharp declines in solar PV costs, which fell by approximately 50 percent between 2000 and 2010. Although past technological advancement and price declines might not continue at the same pace, our goal is to identify a high-stress scenario that captures high penetration of DPV.

Low Electricity Demand Scenario

The QER's Low Electricity Demand scenario departs from the base case in its assumption of lower demand in 2030 and 2050 than in 2010. Overall, the assumptions in this scenario are based on AEO2014's Low Electricity Demand case (EIA, 2014a, p. IF-46).[8]

High Electricity Demand Scenario

The High Electricity Demand scenario is based on the AEO2014 High Economic Growth case. As a consequence, energy consumption and energy use for generating electricity are 5 percent higher in 2030 than in the base case. All other energy and electric power market assumptions are the same as in the Reference case (EIA, 2014a, pp. E-6, A-41).

Greenhouse-Gas Emission Cap + Reduced Demand Scenario

The Greenhouse-Gas Emission Cap + Reduced Demand scenario assumes that total GHG emissions in the United States are reduced by 40 percent. We created it by running NEMS and determining the amount of GHG reduction that occurs in the electricity sector. We then transferred this GHG reduction to ReEDS for the Greenhouse-Gas Emission Cap scenarios. This "medium-low" electricity demand is the electricity demand from the NEMS run that created the Greenhouse-Gas Emission Cap scenario. That demand was used for ReEDS for the scenarios specified here.

Greenhouse-Gas Emission Cap + Reduced Demand + High Nuclear Retirements + High Natural Gas Prices Scenario

In this scenario, we employed the assumptions about high nuclear power retirements and high natural gas prices described in Table 3.1 with the Greenhouse-Gas Emission Cap + Reduced Demand scenario.

Greenhouse-Gas Emission Cap + Reduced Demand + High Renewable-Energy Penetration Scenario

To create this scenario, we combined the assumptions about low wind cost, low solar cost, high PV penetration, and low storage costs described in Table 3.1 with the Greenhouse-Gas Emission Cap and Reduced Demand scenario.

Reduced Demand and High Renewable-Energy Penetration Scenario

This scenario is based on the assumptions about low wind cost, low solar cost, high PV penetration, and low storage costs described in Table 3.1 (High Renewable-Energy Penetration) with Reduced Demand.

---

[8]   The following assumptions underpin this scenario: All of the assumptions of the AEO2014 Best Available Demand Technology scenario for the residential and commercial sectors, including that only the most-efficient equipment of a given year is available for purchase, regardless of cost; building shells increase in efficiency at a faster rate than in the AEO2014 Reference case; distributed electricity generation costs decrease at a faster rate than in the AEO2014 Reference case; and electric motors in industrial equipment have greater efficiencies than in the AEO2014 Reference case.

Policy Options

Three of the combination scenarios in Table 3.1 explicitly include a cap on GHG emissions of 40 percent below 2005 levels to be achieved by 2030. For the other scenarios, we assume that current policy with respect to GHG emissions remains in place. For those cases with GHG caps, we used a reduced-demand profile to mimic the price-responsiveness of consumer demand.

Scenario Analysis

In this section, we compare the consequences of the scenarios in Table 3.1 in terms of demand for new transmission capacity as measured in millions of MW-miles, the cost of new transmission capacity, reductions in GHG emissions, and changes in the cost of electricity. We also address storage and changes in distribution system demand (through assumptions about DPV demand). We then compare model results to the base case, which is based on AEO2014 assumptions.

Variation in Installed Transmission Capacity Across Scenarios

For the 2030 time horizon, the greatest expansion in installed transmission capacity relative to the base case occurs in the Low Wind Cost scenario.[9] In this scenario, total transmission capacity is 13 percent more than the total installed transmission capacity figure employed in the ReEDS model in 2010. Transmission capacity additions in this scenario are 2 percentage points higher than in the base case (Figure 3.4). (The numbers of additional millions of MW-miles of transmission capacity are shown in Figure 3.5.) The least expansion occurs in the High Renewable-Energy Penetration + Reduced Demand scenario, which is 6 percentage points *lower* than in the base case. The difference between relative extremes is 8 percentage points between the High Renewable-Energy Penetration + Reduced Demand and Low Wind Cost scenarios. This significant difference can be explained by the reduction in demand in the High Renewable-Energy Penetration + Reduced Demand case, as well as greater penetration of distributed generation sources closer to consumers. As seen in Figure 3.4, for all but one of the modeled scenarios, the additional transmission capacity installed between 2010 and 2030 is less than 10 million MW-miles.

For a 2050 time horizon (Figure C.1. in Appendix C), the greatest expansion occurs in the Greenhouse-Gas Emission Cap + High Renewable-Energy Penetration + Reduced Demand scenario with total transmission capacity 31 percent higher than the base case. The lowest expansion once again occurs in the High Renewable-Energy Penetration + Reduced Demand scenario with cumulative installed transmission capacity that is 7 percent *lower* than in the base case. The difference between these two extremes is 36 million MW-miles. Increases in the Greenhouse-Gas Emission Cap + High Renewable-Energy Penetration + Reduced Demand scenario are largest in the Northwest, Great Plains, Great Lakes, and Texas. Even with less demand than in the base case, the GHG cap forces more transmission to regions where, like

[9] As noted above, ReEDS models only two-fifths of the transmission system (in 2010, 82.2 million MW-miles out of a total system of 200 million MW-miles (U.S. Department of Energy, 2015c, Chapter 3, p. 52). The figures and percentages cited in this section are based on the 82.2 million MW-miles figure with some comparisons for the entire 200 million MW-mile system.

Figure 3.4
Percentage Changes in Transmission Capacity, by Scenario, 2010 and 2030

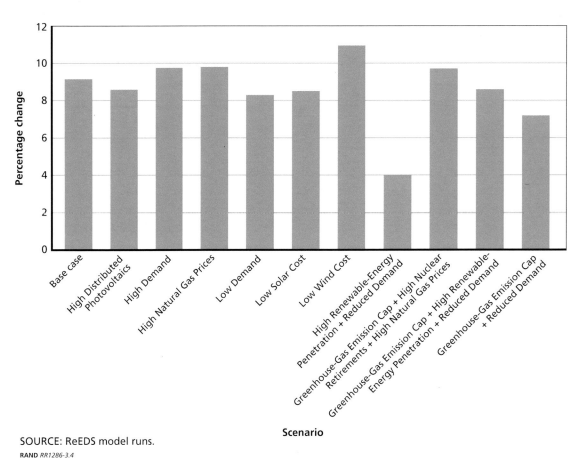

SOURCE: ReEDS model runs.
RAND RR1286-3.4

these, coal-fired plants are retired. Further, greater intermittent renewable capacity imposes higher demand for transmission lines.

Taking total installed transmission capacity as modeled by ReEDS and spreading it uniformly over the 2010–2050 period results in the upper-bound 2030 scenario (Low Wind Cost) having an average annual increase in transmission capacity of approximately 0.6 percent or 546,000 MW-miles per year and the upper-bound 2050 scenario (Greenhouse-Gas Emission Cap + High Renewable-Energy Penetration + Reduced Demand) having an average annual increase in transmission capacity of approximately 1.2 percent, or 1 million MW-miles per year.[10] Even after taking into account that ReEDS models only two-fifths of the transmission system, the projected new capacity needs are lower than recent historical capacity additions.[11]

Total estimated costs (in 2010 dollars) of this newly installed capacity are $23.1 billion ($1.2 billion per year) in the base case and as high as $55.5 billion ($2.8 billion per year) in the

---

[10] The ReEDS model is designed to emphasize endpoint results rather than specific annual build-outs, hence our use of annualized averages.

[11] Based on the Brattle Group's analysis (Chang, Pfeifenberg, and Hagerty, 2013).

Figure 3.5
Additional Installed Transmission Capacity, by Scenario, 2010 and 2030

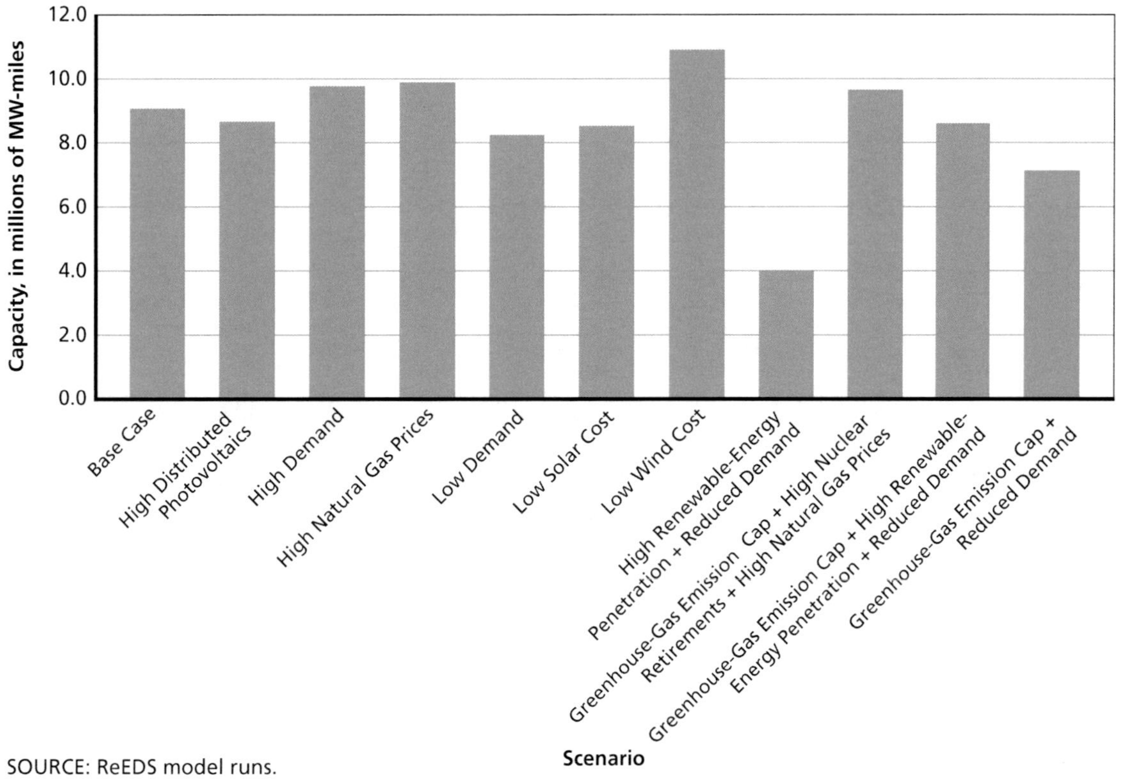

SOURCE: ReEDS model runs.
RAND RR1286-3.5

worst-case scenario.[12] Assuming that intraregional transmission additions remain 60 percent of total transmission costs, this figure suggests total annual expenditures on transmission might range between $3 billion and $7 billion annually.[13] In 2010, the United States installed approximately $10 billion of new capacity, with annual costs ranging from $3 billion to $13 billion (in 2010 dollars) in the past decade.[14]

Transmission Capacity by Region

Figure 3.6 shows *total* transmission capacity by region for the base case and two scenarios with the highest and lowest total installed capacity. Differences across scenarios and between regions relative to the base case are within the bounds of model error and therefore not significant. More-significant build-outs occur by 2050, according to the model runs, and a clear difference emerges among the scenarios by 2050, as shown in Appendix C.

At the regional level, there is relatively little variation in installed transmission capacity across the scenarios that generate the highest and lowest levels of additional capacity between 2010 and 2030. The highest is the Great Lakes region, with roughly a 15-percent difference

---

[12] As noted above, ReEDS models only two-fifths of the transmission system (in 2010, 82.2 million MW-miles out of a total system of 200 million MW-miles (U.S. Department of Energy, 2015c, Chapter 3, p. 52).

[13] Based on the Brattle Group's analysis (Chang, Pfeifenberg, and Hagerty, 2013).

[14] We note that these cost calculations might not be using consistent assumptions (e.g., inclusion of operation and maintenance costs).

Figure 3.6
U.S. Transmission Capacity, by Region and Scenario, 2030

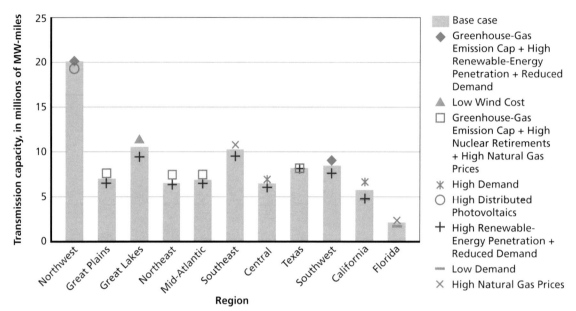

SOURCE: ReEDS model runs.
NOTE: The bar represents the base case. Scenarios that generated the highest and lowest values in each region are represented by their symbols.
RAND *RR1286-3.6*

between the maximum and minimum scenarios for *total capacity*, which reflects nearly a 100-percent difference between the maximum and minimum additional capacity. For most scenarios for regions, the difference between maximum and minimum additional capacity is less than 1 million MW-miles. The results look different, however, in the 2050 time horizon. There are notable differences between the highest and lowest installed transmission capacity across the explored scenario for the following regions: Northwest, Great Plains, Great Lakes, Southeast, Central, and Texas. For four out of those six regions (all but the Southeast and Central), the primary driver of the transmission expansion is the 40-percent cap on GHG emissions, the corresponding decline in electricity generated by coal-fired power plants, and the increased use of renewable energy.

Among these six regions in 2050, the greatest difference between the highest and lowest transmission builds occurs in the Great Lakes region. The Greenhouse-Gas Emission Cap + High Renewable-Energy Penetration + Reduced Demand scenario calls for the greatest expansion in transmission capacity, which is driven by dramatic reductions in coal-fired generation and significant increases in wind capacity. The High Renewable-Energy Penetration + Reduced Demand scenario results in the lowest expansion of transmission lines, although the expansion is not significantly different from the base case in 2050, as shown in Figure C.1 in Appendix C.

Effects of Wind and Solar on Transmission, by Region

Although assumptions of low solar and wind cost lead to increased solar and wind capacity, neither has an appreciable effect on transmission capacity in 2030 compared to the base case.

Figure 3.7
Additions to U.S. Transmission Capacity, by Region and Scenario, 2030

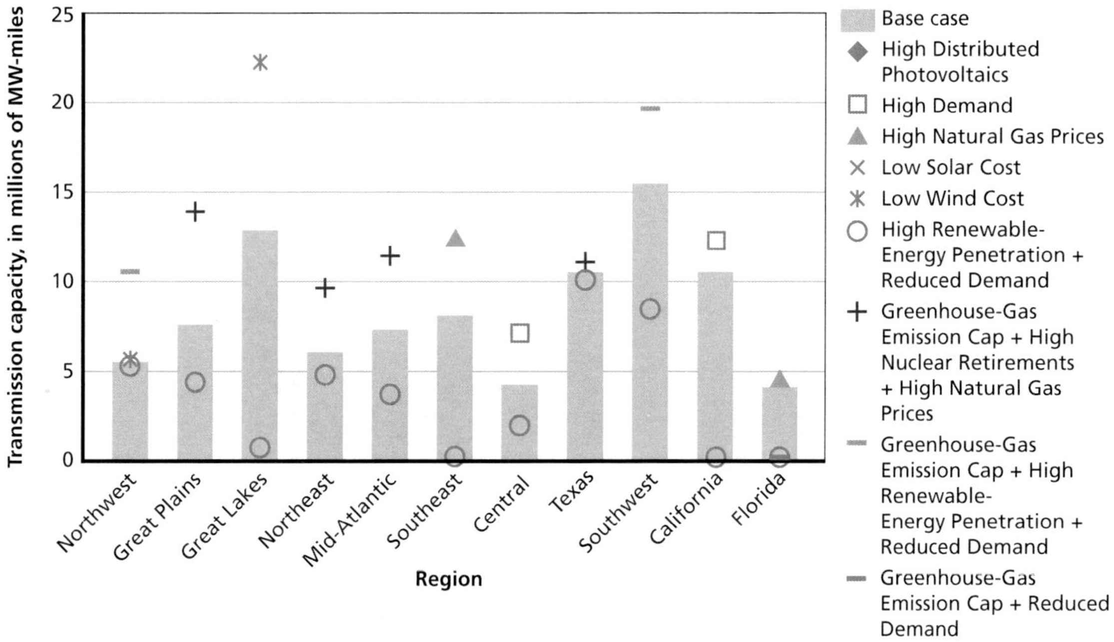

SOURCE: ReEDS model runs.
NOTE: The bar represents the base case. Scenarios that generated the highest and lowest values in each region are represented by their symbols.
RAND *RR1286-3.7*

Total transmission capacity is marginally higher under the Low Wind Cost scenario than the Low Solar Cost scenario (2 percent), but neither scenario differs from the base case substantially in terms of increased construction of transmission capacity, particularly in light of the uncertainties in model assumptions. Total transmission capacity in the Low Solar Cost scenario is actually *lower* than in the base case (–1 percent) (Figure 3.8). This result holds at the regional level, with modest transmission increases occurring only in the Great Lakes (9 percent) and Great Plains (6 percent) regions, and then only for the Low Wind Cost scenario (Figure 3.9).[15]

The model results suggest that only limited additional transmission capacity is required under low renewable technology–cost scenarios. As seen in Figure 3.10, the ReEDS model shows relatively modest changes in intraregional capacity, suggesting futures in which renewable costs fall and capacity increases are unlikely to necessitate substantially more construction of new transmission than has taken place in recent years.

Greenhouse-Gas Reductions Across Cases With and Without Caps

The largest GHG reductions achieved without imposing constraints on emissions occur from the combination scenario, High Renewable-Energy Penetration + Reduced Demand, which assumes favorable demand and technology costs. This scenario achieves approximately 3.5 billion tons of cumulative incremental reductions in emissions of GHGs between 2010 and 2030 compared to the base case. This is a reduction of approximately 16 percent from within the

---

[15] In 2020, no region sees a 1-percent or greater increase in transmission capacity.

Figure 3.8
Comparison of Transmission Capacity Between the Low Wind Cost and Low Solar Cost Scenarios, 2030

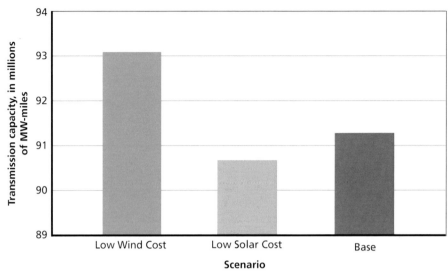

SOURCE: ReEDS model runs.
RAND RR1286-3.8

Figure 3.9
Comparison of Total Transmission Build-Outs Between the Low Wind Cost and Low Solar Cost Scenarios, by Originating Region, 2030

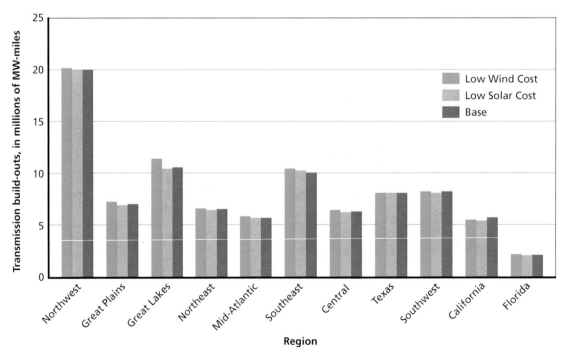

SOURCE: ReEDS model runs.
RAND RR1286-3.9

Figure 3.10
Comparison of Transmission Build-Outs Between the Low Wind Cost and Low Solar Cost Scenarios Only Within Regions, 2030

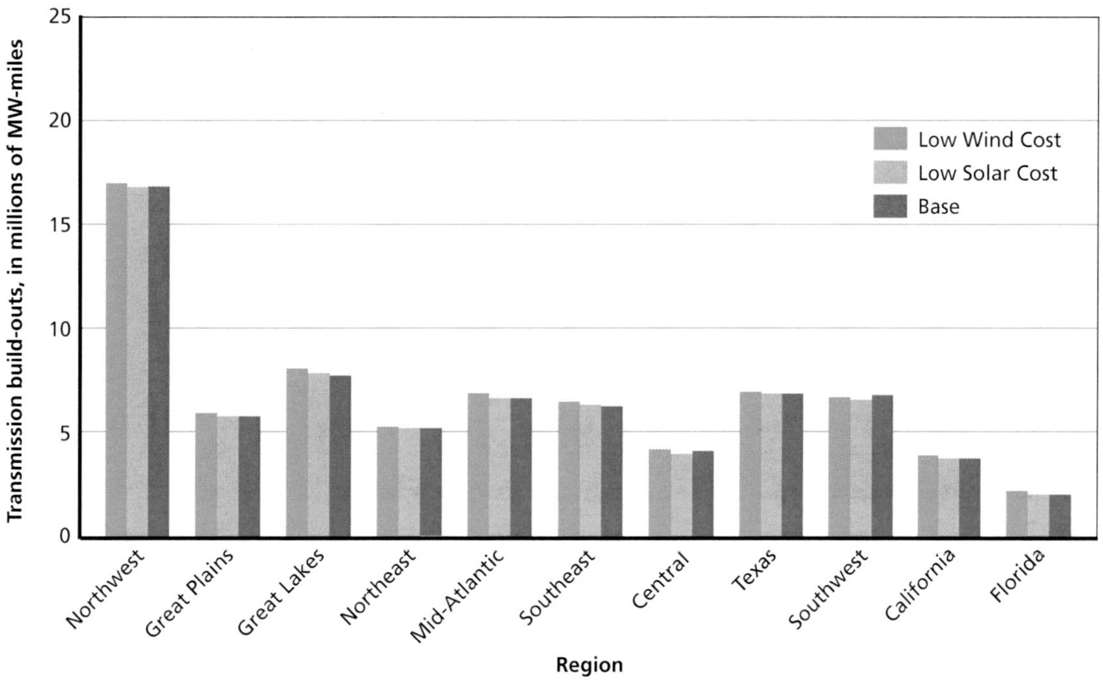

SOURCE: ReEDS model runs.
NOTE: The model results shown here are a subset of the results shown in Figure 3.9. The version of ReEDS used for these analyses models only spur lines for CSP and wind. Intraregional build-outs include only these spur lines; they do not represent, for example, lines connecting two cities within a same region.
RAND *RR1286-3.10*

electricity sector. The Greenhouse-Gas Emission Cap + Reduced Demand scenario, which imposes an economy-wide reduction in annual emissions of 40 percent by 2030, reduces cumulative emissions to approximately 16.5 billion tons, or approximately 6 billion tons below those in the 2030 base case, a 27-percent reduction. The gap between cap and noncap scenarios is 2.5 billion tons through 2030. By 2050, the gap increases to approximately 15 billion tons.

Factors and Policies That Would Result in Reduced Greenhouse-Gas Emissions Without Substantial Cost Increases

The ReEDS model analyses suggest that a future U.S. electricity system could see widely different levels of GHG emissions depending on what transpires with technology, energy prices, and policies. Most scenarios yield, at most, modest increases in electricity prices. Figure 3.12 shows electricity prices in 2010 dollars and cumulative GHG emissions (in billions of tons) for all single-factor cases and combinations. Points in the upper right have both higher prices and larger emissions, while points in the lower left reflect scenarios in which both prices and emissions are relatively low. Most scenarios without strict limits on GHGs achieve only modest reductions in emissions. To achieve more-substantial emission reductions under our modeled cases, however, requires policies directly focused on reducing emissions, such as the modeled 40-percent economy-wide GHG cap.

Figure 3.12 shows the performance of scenarios relative to the base case. In the base case, annual CO_2 emissions from the electricity sector are 2 percent lower in 2030 than in 2010.

Figure 3.11
Comparison of Greenhouse-Gas Emissions in the Power Sector Among the Base Case, the Greenhouse-Gas Emission Cap + Reduced Demand Scenario, and High Renewable-Energy Penetration + Reduced Demand Scenario

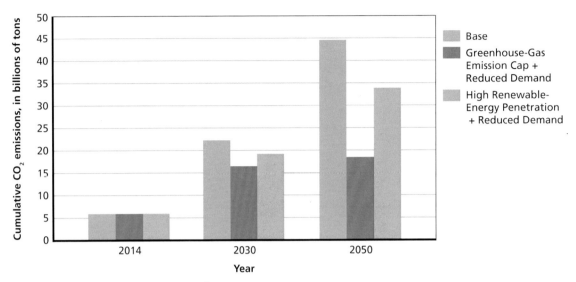

SOURCE: ReEDS model runs; base year of 2005.
RAND *RR1286-3.11*

The largest GHG reductions achieved without imposing constraints on emissions occur from the combination scenario, High Renewable-Energy Penetration + Reduced Demand, which assumes favorable demand and technology costs. In this scenario, annual CO_2 emissions from the electricity sector in 2030 are 28 percent lower than in 2010. In contrast, all scenarios that include caps on emissions reduce annual CO_2 emissions in the electricity sector by 64 percent between 2010 and 2030. This gap between capped and uncapped scenarios underscores the critical role of aggressive coal retirements in reducing emissions. Further, even under the most stressful scenario we tested of reduced availability of conventional sources, the Greenhouse-Gas Emission Cap + Nuclear Retirements + High Natural Gas Prices scenario, the 64-percent reduction in CO_2 emissions is accompanied by increased costs to consumers of only around 6 percent. As with all of these scenarios, we cannot say definitively which are more likely to occur, hence the caveat to not take the distribution of performance among the scenarios shown in Figure 3.12 as an indicator of likelihood.

Electricity Price Changes Under Different Scenarios

In both the 2030 (Figure 3.13) and 2050 (Figure C.5 in Appendix C) time horizons, the highest average price is found in the Greenhouse-Gas Emission Cap + Nuclear Retirement + High Natural Gas Prices scenario. In 2030, the highest electricity price is $0.108 per kilowatt-hour (6 percent higher than in the base case), and, in 2050, the highest price is $0.115 per kilowatt-hour (7 percent higher than in the base case), although our results should not be interpreted to imply a high level of precision or that relatively low price increases are the most likely outcome.

The price results across all ReEDS runs are similar to historical average prices in the United States. Between 2004 and 2013, the annual average electricity price in the United States across all sectors was $0.095 per kilowatt-hour, ranging from $0.088 per kilowatt-hour

Figure 3.12
Comparison of Greenhouse-Gas Emissions and Electricity Prices Across All Scenarios to 2030

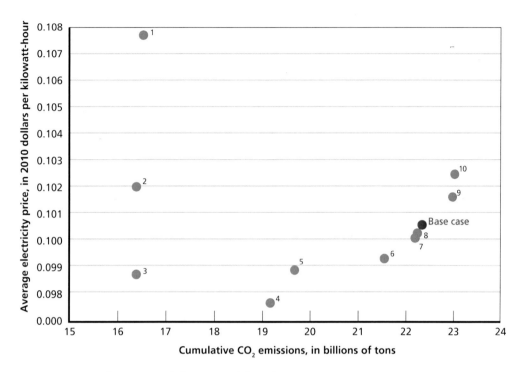

1 Greenhouse-Gas Emission Cap + High Nuclear
   Retirements + High Natural Gas Prices
2 Greenhouse-Gas Emission Cap + Reduced Demand
3 Greenhouse-Gas Emission Cap + High Renewable-
   Energy Penetration + Reduced Demand
4 Greenhouse-Gas Emission Cap + Reduced Demand

5 Low Demand
6 Low Wind Cost
7 Low Solar Cost
8 High Distributed Photovoltaics
9 High Demand
10 High Natural Gas Prices

SOURCE: ReEDS model runs.
RAND RR1286-3.12

in 2004 to $0.094 per kilowatt-hour in 2013.[16] The ReEDS scenario that results in the highest price in 2030 ($0.108 per kilowatt-hour) is approximately 14 percent higher than the average price between 2004 and 2013. These price effects are broadly consistent with other models, including the results from a recent industry-sponsored analysis, which estimated that average electricity prices would rise by approximately 12 percent over baseline during the 2017–2030 period as a result of the proposed Clean Power Plan (National Economic Research Associates Economic Consulting, 2014, p. S-6). ReEDS-modeled prices are also in line with results from a SWITCH scenario-based analysis of the Western Electricity Coordinating Council system, which estimated that, under a GHG-reduction scenario, prices in 2030 would range from $0.110 per kilowatt-hour and $0.114 per kilowatt-hour (Nelson et al., 2012, pp. 436–447).

---

[16] All prices are in 2010 dollars, drawn from EIA, 2015.

Figure 3.13
Comparison of Electricity Prices Across All Scenarios to 2030

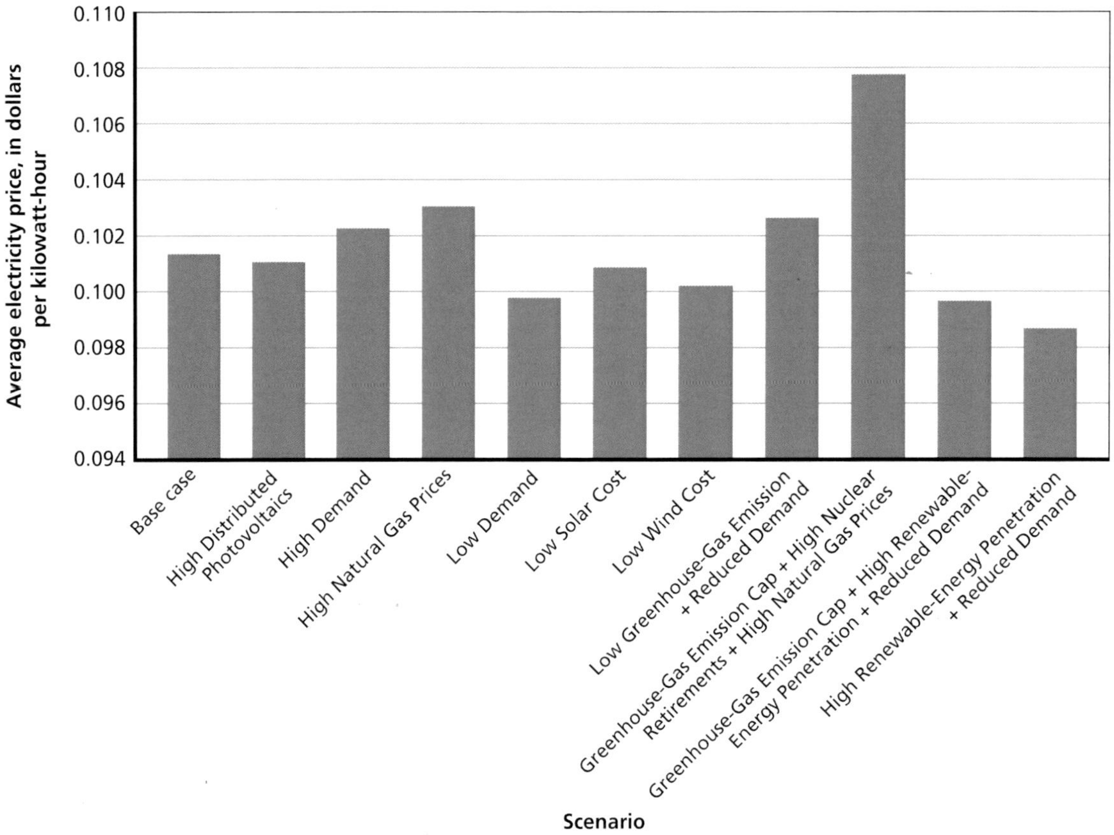

SOURCE: ReEDS model runs.

RAND *RR1286-3.13*

Prices, Transmission Capacity, and Greenhouse Gases Under Best- and Worst-Case Scenarios for Cost-Effective Greenhouse-Gas Reductions

We used ReEDS to run two scenarios that represent the best and worst conditions from the perspective of the underlying individual stress factors. The combination scenario Greenhouse-Gas Emission Cap + High Nuclear Retirements + High Natural Gas Prices includes the 40-percent GHG cap, high natural gas prices, and high nuclear retirements; together, these constitute a less appealing future, given relatively high costs, but do result in significant GHG reductions. In the scenario Greenhouse-Gas Emission Cap + High Renewable-Energy Penetration + Reduced Demand, the GHG cap is combined with low renewable-resource costs and low electricity demand. This is a more optimistic future, in which conditions are favorable to achieving significant reductions in GHG emissions.

Because both scenarios include caps on emissions, total emission reductions by 2030 are the same. However, implications for electricity costs are quite different. The Greenhouse-Gas Emission Cap + High Nuclear Retirements + High Natural Gas Prices scenario generates the highest modeled electricity costs, at $0.108 per kilowatt-hour, while the Greenhouse-Gas Emission Cap + High Renewable-Energy Penetration + Reduced Demand scenario achieves some of the lowest electricity costs across all scenarios, at just under $0.10 per kilowatt-hour. Neither combination scenario puts significant pressure on the transmission system. Although

Greenhouse-Gas Emission Cap + High Nuclear Retirements + High Natural Gas Prices results in higher transmission additions than the base case and Greenhouse-Gas Emission Cap + High Renewable-Energy Penetration + Reduced Demand produces lower added transmission capacity than the base case, neither deviates from the base case in terms of new transmissions build-outs by more than 5 percent.

Role, Drivers, and Influence of Electricity Storage

We briefly discuss storage as modeled in ReEDS, although we note that the ReEDS model structure does not capture the full value of storage and could lead to underestimates in new capacity.[17] Under the base case, ReEDS estimates that total installed storage capacity will be approximately 22 GW in 2030, which implies almost no new additions to storage over the 2010–2030 period. Most individual scenarios similarly result in little additional storage capacity, even for scenarios in which technology costs fall for intermittent renewable sources (i.e., wind and solar) and even in the case when storage costs were low. Only scenarios that include GHG caps lead to substantial additional storage capacity. The Greenhouse-Gas Emission Cap + High Nuclear Retirements + High Natural Gas Prices and Greenhouse-Gas Emission Cap + High Renewable-Energy Penetration + Reduced Demand scenarios each see additional storage capacity of approximately 40 percent over the base case. The cap induces additional installed wind and solar capacity, leading to some increases in storage to mitigate effects of intermittency.

Resilience

As in Chapter Two, our discussion of power grid resilience was not informed by modeling results but rather a literature review by RAND researchers (Willis and Loa, 2015). Despite the best efforts of system operators and the engineers they employ, electricity grids sometimes fail. Extreme weather events, operator errors, premeditated physical or cyberattacks, and other disruptions lead to power outages of varying severity. Depending on the cause of the outage, consequences can range from short disruptions of electrical service, such as loss of power in a neighborhood caused by the failure of a transformer, to long-duration blackouts affecting an entire region, such as the 2003 cascading outage that affected the Northeastern United States and Canada.

The grid can be made more resilient to unanticipated outages in several ways, including by (1) making it more robust through investments in self-supporting transmission tower structures to prevent domino collapse, advanced monitoring and control systems, protective substation barriers, and enhanced personnel security; (2) accelerating recovery from an outage by adding more linemen, stocking more transformers and other equipment, improving information on locations of outages, and other such measures; or (3) improving society's ability to cope with the effects of disruptions to electric service by purchases of generators or measures to reduce reliance on power from the grid for key functions (National Research Council of the National Academies, 2012; Electric Power Research Institute, 2013; GridWise Alliance, 2013).

---

[17] ReEDS does not model the distribution grid and is therefore not capable of capturing the value of storage on the distribution system. Also, ReEDS represents each day using four time slices, which inherently smooths some of the arbitrage opportunities that make storage more attractive.

Figure 3.14
Installed Storage Capacity in 2030

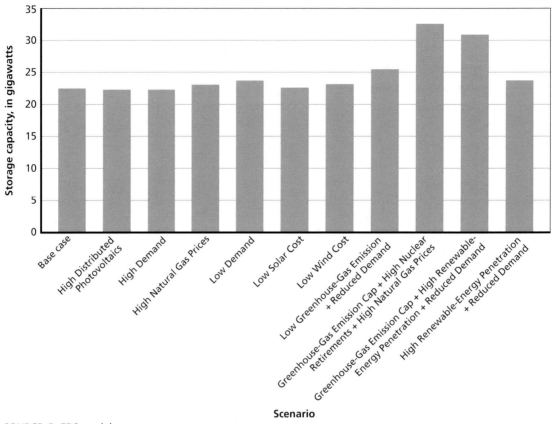

SOURCE: ReEDS model runs.
RAND *RR1286-3.14*

Government plays an important role on both the prevention and recovery sides of increasing resilience. The U.S. Department of Energy funds several research and development (R&D) projects targeted at increasing system efficiency, reliability, and resilience. As demonstrated by restoration and recovery efforts by federal, state, and local agencies—along with the utilities— following Hurricane Sandy, government support is a vital component of overall efforts to ensure health and safety in the aftermath of major catastrophes.

Recovery times for local outages are typically on the order of minutes or hours, although derecho-related power outages result in notably longer restoration times (Hines, Apt, and Talukdar, 2009). To reduce the more standard-type outages, utilities trim threatening tree limbs, increase underground installation of lines, reinforce overhead lines, and invest in reconfigurable distribution feeders. Utilities and public service commissions have to balance the cost of these measures against the expected reduction in outages when evaluating measures to reduce local outages.

Long-duration outages over large geographic areas are much less frequent than local outages, but, when they do occur, they have serious impacts. These disruptions can be triggered by storms, such as the 1998 Quebec ice storm, shorts on major transmission lines, or potentially through a coordinated attack on the power grid by a savvy adversary. These types of outages inflict huge economic losses and disrupt critical services that depend on electricity (Council of

Economic Advisers and U.S. Department of Energy Office of Electricity Delivery and Energy Reliability, 2013).

Planning for and recovering from these types of outages can be a much more difficult task. The events that precipitate such outages are hard to predict, making planning difficult. They typically result from failures in the transmission system, which take more time to repair than distribution systems. Unplanned shutdown of nuclear plants can also be problematic when these events occur, although plants are required to have substantial redundancy and independence in their transmission circuits (International Atomic Energy Agency, 2009).

Some events could disrupt the entire U.S. grid, leading to huge costs to U.S. citizens. Scientists, engineers, and policymakers have examined the likelihood and potential effects of a severe geomagnetic storm resulting from a solar storm. Such a storm could induce large current flows that might severely damage high-voltage transformers, leading to voltage collapse and resulting in a nationwide power outage. NERC's GridEx II exercise has investigated whether a targeted cyberattack on the entire U.S. grid could lead to the same outcome. In its after-action report, NERC noted the continued need to improve and increase information-sharing and coordination, consider scenarios of simultaneous attack, improve incident response, and improve situational awareness (NERC, 2014).

Steps can be taken to protect the grid from solar storms or cyberattacks. In the case of geomagnetic storms, adding series capacitors to block geomagnetically induced currents or neutral-current blocking devices to the system would limit the damage. But these technologies tend to be costly, and there is little consensus on the magnitude or likelihood of such a storm. Estimates of the likelihood of a severe solar storm fall in the range of 0.2 to 1 percent per year (Nuclear Regulatory Commission, 2012; Royal Academy of Engineering, 2013).

Technology options for mitigating disruptions of all types, but especially suited for widespread and long-duration blackouts, are available. For instance, microgrids that can be isolated from the larger grid in the event of a regional or national blackout could be used to ensure that key users, such as grocery stores, schools, and police stations, continue to have access to power. These microgrids with marginal system upgrades would harness distributed generation, distribution automation, controls, and advanced metering infrastructure to deliver power to select critical users, although there is a range of options for how the process of selecting critical users would work in practice (Narayanan and Morgan, 2012, pp. 1183–1193). Microgrids have received federal support primarily in the form of R&D funding in such areas as planning, design, operations, and control of microgrids. But the legislative and regulatory environment makes the creation of microgrids complicated and, in some instances, prohibitive in much of the United States. For example, public service commissions have not sorted out how to regulate microgrids competitively with larger entities that can capture economies of scale (Hempling, 2013, p. 412). Utilities and their state public utility commissions seek a balance between increasing resilience of their systems and ratepayers' concerns about affordability. In the end, whether the proposed investments are in microgrids or other measures, benefit–cost analyses are needed that appropriately value the near- and longer-term costs of regional disruptions and the benefits of more-rapid reconstitution of a disabled system (Honorable, 2014).

Key Findings

- According to the ReEDS model analysis, by 2030, the United States will need an addition of between 5 and 13 percent over 2010 installed capacity of 82 million MW-miles.
- By 2050, a delayed build-out of the transmission system is projected under the Greenhouse-Gas Emission Cap + High Renewable-Energy Penetration + Reduced Demand scenario, and the lowest expansion occurs in the High Renewable-Energy Penetration + Reduced Demand scenario. Even with lower demand than in the base case, the GHG cap forces more transmission to regions where coal-fired plants are retired. Greater intermittent renewable capacity imposes higher demand for transmission lines.
- Total costs of installing the new transmission capacity are commensurate with historical yearly investments.
- The projected new capacity needs are lower than recent historical capacity additions. In 2010, the United States installed approximately $10 billion of new capacity, with annual installation costs ranging from $3 billion to $13 billion in the past decade.[18]
- Projected capacity additions are not associated with increases in electricity prices that are significantly different from recent historical changes or predicted increases from other modeling efforts.

---

[18] Based on the Brattle Group's analysis of Federal Energy Regulatory Commission Form 1 data compiled in Ventyx's Velocity Suite (Chang, Pfeifenberg, and Hagerty, 2013).

We note that these cost calculations might not be using consistent assumptions (e.g., inclusion of operation and maintenance costs).

CHAPTER FOUR

Natural Gas

Natural gas production in the United States has been rising sharply since the mid-2000s, growing from 23 trillion cubic feet (Tcf) in 2005 to more than 31 Tcf in 2014 (Figure 4.1). Shale gas development, primarily in the Marcellus region, has driven domestic total natural gas production to all-time highs, driving down prices and prompting policy discussions about how to use newly available supplies. Under the AEO2014 Reference case, natural gas production could reach 34 Tcf annually by 2030, an increase of 43 percent over 2012 levels of 24 Tcf. Dry natural gas production under the High Oil and Gas Resource case is 5 Tcf higher; at 39 Tcf, this projection is 62 percent more than 2012 levels (EIA, 2014a, p. D-15).

To collect, transport, and distribute this natural gas, the U.S. TS&D system might have to be expanded. Substantial increases in production, especially in areas of the country that have historically not produced at such high levels, will require investment in feeder pipelines to connect to the wider natural gas pipeline system. Depending on how new gas supplies are

Figure 4.1
U.S. Gross Withdrawals of Natural Gas, 1967 to 2013

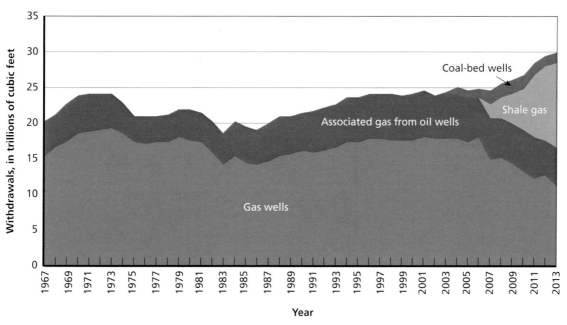

SOURCE: EIA, 2013d.
RAND RR1286-4.1

used, large-scale transmission pipelines or conversion of existing pipelines (i.e., to reverse flow direction) could be required as well.

Key Issues

The degree of pipeline capacity expansion will depend on the amount and location of gas production and where gas supplies are consumed. For example, in a future with a sizable amount of liquefied natural gas (LNG) exports, increased pipeline capacity would be needed to move gas to exporting regions, primarily the Gulf Coast but also the East Coast. Additionally, if lower natural gas prices drive continued increases in consumption from electric power or from industry, a different configuration of pipelines would move supplies to demand centers. In particular, if U.S. government policy encourages the use of natural gas for transportation, increased demand for natural gas from this sector could affect demand for new pipelines and their location.[1]

Performance Metrics

We sought to identify the conditions that have the greatest potential to stress the natural gas TS&D system. Accordingly, our analysis focused on two outcome metrics, which capture core characteristics of the U.S. natural gas TS&D system through the year 2030. These metrics are demand for new transmission and cost of new transmission. We also assessed U.S. industry's capacity to build new pipelines.

Model and Data

We worked with EPSA to identify stressing factors and analyze results from a set of natural gas–sector modeling runs, which Deloitte MarketPoint carried out using its World Gas model. Appendix A provides a summary of the model characteristics.

Key Uncertainties

We identified scenarios that reflect different futures for U.S. natural gas production and used them to assess the potential stresses on the U.S. natural gas TS&D system. In particular, we focused on the potential need for and cost of new pipeline capacity in the context of differing levels of consumption and prices among plausible futures. Table 4.1 summarizes the scenarios employed.

---

[1] EPSA conducted its own analysis of resilience in the natural gas TS&D system.

Table 4.1
Natural Gas Scenarios

Scenario	Parameters Varied	Value	Description
Base case	N/A	N/A	Base case built around AEO2014 Reference case
High U.S. Demand			We assume high domestic demand for natural gas across all sectors (except residential), driven by sector growth and pressure from carbon prices
	Carbon price, in dollars per ton	25[a]	
	Coal retirements, in gigawatts	104	This assumption is broadly consistent with ReEDS used for the analysis in Chapter Three. In 2030, ReEDS assumes 76 GW of retirements and does not reach 104 GW in the base case until 2040.
	High industrial growth	AEO2014 High Economic Growth case	
	High transport demand	RAND-specified	
High U.S. Exports of LNG	LNG export capacity by 2030, in billions of cubic feet per day	20.4[b]	We assume substantial growth in LNG export capacity in the Gulf region consistent with strong international demand and conducive U.S. policy. In comparison, the base case assumes 9.1 Bcfd in total export capacity.
High Global Supply	Shale gas capital costs, as a percentage reduced from the base case	30	We assume higher global production of natural gas, driven by increased gas output outside of the United States, including shale gas.

SOURCES: EIA, 2014a; Deloitte MarketPoint World Gas model (see Deloitte MarketPoint, undated).

NOTE: Bcfd = billions of cubic feet per day.

[a] The carbon price increases at 5 percent per year, beginning in 2020 at a starting price of $31.91 and climbing to $51.97 by 2050.

[b] Export capacity is concentrated in Texas and Louisiana; note that this is an extreme stretch or bounding case and is not necessarily considered to be likely.

Scenario Analysis

Circumstances for Increasing Pipeline Capacity

Under the base-case scenario, modeled pipeline capacity additions are approximately 37 Bcfd between 2015 and 2030 (Figure 4.2). The High U.S. Demand scenario results in total capacity additions of 50.7 Bcfd between 2015 and 2030. The largest increase occurs in the High U.S. Exports of LNG scenario, with total capacity additions of 76.5 Bcfd by 2030. At roughly double the pipeline capacity expansion called for under the base case, the High U.S. Exports of LNG scenario would require major additional investments.

Relative to recent capacity expansions, none of these scenarios appears particularly challenging. Between 1998 and 2008, total natural gas pipeline capacity in the United States increased by 9.7 Bcfd per year, or a total expansion of approximately 20,000 miles of pipeline (Tobin, 2008). In comparison, the base-case scenario results in an average additional capacity of 2.5 Bcfd per year, while the High U.S. Exports of LNG scenario yields 5.1 Bcfd per year. In short, the rate of capacity expansion in 1998 and 2008 was roughly double that predicted under even the most extreme modeled scenario.

Figure 4.2
Total Pipeline Capacity Additions, 2015 to 2030

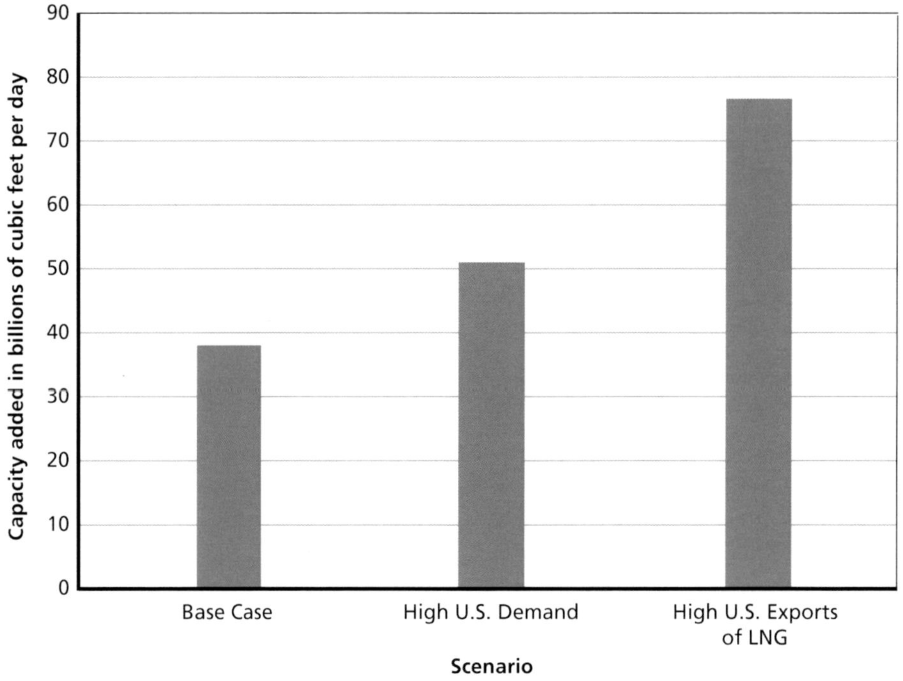

SOURCE: Deloitte MarketPoint, undated.
RAND *RR1286-4.2*

Estimated Cost of Pipeline Capacity Additions

The total private costs of constructing added natural gas pipeline capacity depends on many factors, including the state or region in which the pipeline is built and the specific geography involved, the pipe diameter, and the number of pipeline miles. Assuming a 20-inch average pipe diameter and average national costs per mile for this size pipe, the 18,760 miles of pipeline estimated under the base case would cost approximately $1.8 million per mile to construct (Ortiz, Samaras, and Molina-Perez, 2013, p. 14) or $33.5 billion in 2010 dollars. Under the High U.S. Demand scenario, reversing flows of existing pipelines would result in fewer miles of new pipeline built than in the High U.S. Exports of LNG scenario. Pipeline reversals would reduce costs of building new pipelines below those projected in the High U.S. Exports of LNG scenario.[2] Pipeline construction would run 17,646 miles and cost approximately $31.5 billion, $24 billion less than in the High U.S. Exports of LNG scenario.

Capacity Expansion, by Region

Across all scenarios, the Marcellus region generally experiences the largest increases in pipeline capacity, ranging from 9.2 Bcfd in the base case to 10.9 Bcfd in the High U.S. Demand scenario. Other regions see relatively small baseline capacity additions, but, under alternative scenarios, some do experience major additions. For example, in the Southeast region, pipeline capacity grows by 1.4 Bcfd in the base case, but, under the High U.S. Exports of LNG sce-

---

[2] For example, in early 2014, 1.6 Bcfd of natural gas was moving from the Utica and Marcellus production areas using pipeline reversals ("Natural Gas to Exit Appalachia on Reversed Mainline Pipes," 2014).

nario, the model predicts an additional 9.8 Bcfd of expansion. The San Juan/Permian, Gulf, and Mid-Atlantic to West regions are projected to need approximately 5 Bcfd of additional capacity under the base case, but only the Gulf region sees substantial additional capacity under alternative scenarios. New pipeline capacity in the Gulf region runs 18.8 Bcfd in the High U.S. Exports of LNG scenario. In contrast, the Mid-Atlantic to West region sees less additional capacity in both the High U.S. Demand and High U.S. Exports of LNG scenarios than in the base case. Although some of the capacity additions are larger than in the base case, none is particularly large compared with historical capacity additions.

Projections of Pipeline Utilization

Under the assumptions of the base case, national pipeline utilization rates rise from approximately 50 percent to 62 percent between 2015 and 2030. The alternative scenarios show similar increases for the same period, with the High U.S. Demand and High U.S. Exports of LNG scenarios reaching 67- and 66-percent capacity utilization rates by 2030, respectively. At the national level, none of the alternative scenarios results in significantly higher pipeline capacity utilization rates than the base case. Existing excess pipeline capacity helps explain why the model predicts relatively modest increases in new installation of capacity for 2015 through 2030.

Pipeline capacity utilization rates vary more at the regional level than at the national level, but deviations from the base case are still small. The East region is projected to have a capac-

Figure 4.3
National Natural Gas Pipeline Capacity Utilization Rates, 2015 to 2030

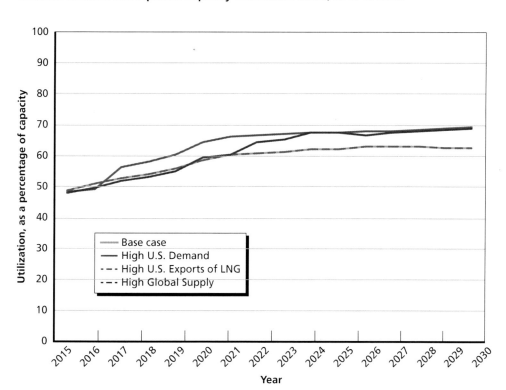

SOURCE: Deloitte MarketPoint World Gas model.

ity utilization rate of approximately 76 percent of pipeline capacity in all scenarios, and the Midwest and West regions are almost as stable, below 50 percent and above 80 percent, respectively. In contrast, utilization in the Gulf region is 56 percent of pipeline capacity in the base case but rises to 62 and 75 percent in the High U.S. Demand and High U.S. Exports of LNG scenarios, respectively. Utilization is highest in the South region in the High U.S. Demand scenario, reaching 62 percent in 2030, higher than the 51 percent in the base case.

Key Findings

- Additions to natural gas pipelines under all cases are modest, less than recent additions.
- Increased capacity utilization plays a key role in mitigating demand for new pipelines.
- Reversing pipeline flows also play a role in restraining new-pipeline construction as sources of supply and demand shift.
- In all of the scenarios examined, normal pipeline expansion and construction practices should be adequate to meet the demand for new pipeline.
- With modest demand for new pipeline capacity, we foresee few pressures that would increase the cost of building pipelines.

Implications for Energy Investments and Policy

In the preceding chapters, we show that, from a national perspective, U.S. TS&D systems are likely to be relatively robust between now and 2030 under slow-moving stress cases. Potential future stresses on the various TS&D systems examined in this analysis will be regional in nature. However, some vulnerabilities within regions do exist and will require policy attention. We also looked at the resilience of the three TS&D systems and identified events in which regional disruptions would be possible. In no instance, however, did we identify a plausible scenario that would lead to prolonged systemic outages of these systems at a national scale.

Petroleum and Refined-Oil Products

The analysis in Chapter Two indicates that potential future stresses on the various TS&D systems examined in this analysis will be regional in nature. The most-immediate stress is on the railroads that transport oil out of the Bakken, Eagle Ford, and Permian basins. Pipelines are being built in these basins to link them to the mid-American pipeline systems that serve the Midwest and South Central United States. However, in the interim, large volumes of oil are being transported by rail, causing substantial congestion on rail systems, especially in the Upper Midwest. To reduce this congestion, additional pipelines will be needed to move oil out of these basins, connecting them more fully to the midcontinent system.

Under most scenarios, currently planned additions to pipeline capacity, coupled with existing use of rail, should be sufficient to handle projected increases in output. However, in the High Resource scenario with a continued ban on exports, a combination of lack of demand for tight light crude and constraints on railroad capacity could lead to shutting in some production.

The very large cost differentials between hauling crude by rail versus pipeline (two or three times) will lead to continued expansion in crude-oil pipeline capacity. However, large-scale use of rail to transport crude oil is likely here to stay because of the flexibility that rail provides.

Spillage is generally lower when transporting oil by rail than by pipeline, but several high-profile incidents have raised public concern about transport by rail. In the event of another major derailment, especially one involving loss of life, government authorities could impose a moratorium on all rail shipments until safety procedures were reviewed and improved. As long as such a moratorium is in place, it would severely affect production in the Bakken.

Implications for Resilience

The crude-oil and refined-oil product TS&D systems are robust in the face of disruptive events. Even in the event of substantial damage to the system, such as an earthquake in southern California or terrorist attack that would severely damage refineries and import terminals in that region, supplies would flow relatively soon after the event, albeit at a cost in terms of higher prices at the pump (Meade and Molander, 2006).

Electric Power

In none of our scenarios for the electricity TS&D system did we find problems in building, at reasonable cost, the additional transmission that would be needed. We did find that demand for new transmission was highest in the Low Wind Cost scenario, but, even in that scenario, demand for new transmission lines would not be difficult for current industry to satisfy. What could be challenging could be the need for improved grid operations to manage a much more decentralized and distributed generation system, were that scenario to come to pass.

Implications for Resilience

Extreme weather events, operator errors, premeditated physical or cyberattacks, and other disruptions can lead to power outages of varying severity. Recovery times for local outages are typically on the order of minutes or hours, although some areas do experience outages of one or more days; at the national scale, the effects tend to be small. Utilities and public service commissions balance the costs of measures to reduce outages against the expected value of reductions in outages.

Long-duration outages over large geographic areas are much less frequent than local outages, but, when they do occur, they have serious impacts. For example, a severe geomagnetic storm could induce large current flows that might severely damage high-voltage transformers, leading to voltage collapse, resulting in a nationwide power outage (Royal Academy of Engineering, 2013). A targeted cyberattack on the entire U.S. grid could potentially lead to the same outcome. Steps can be taken to protect the grid from solar storms or cyberattacks, but the necessary technologies tend to be costly, and the actual risk is poorly understood. Utilities and public service commissions often debate approval of measures to mitigate these risks because their value to ratepayers can be difficult to reconcile in the context of low-frequency, disruptive events. Federal guidance on valuable resilience-enhancing measures could enhance progress.

Natural Gas

To collect, transport, and distribute increased supplies of natural gas, the U.S. TS&D system will have to be expanded. The extent of pipeline capacity expansion will depend on the amount of gas produced, its location, and the locations where gas supplies are consumed. In a future in which the U.S. government facilitates exports of sizable amounts of LNG, increased pipeline capacity would be needed to move gas to exporting regions, primarily the Gulf Coast but also the East Coast and coastal Canada. If lower natural gas prices drive continued increases in consumption, different configurations of pipelines could be needed to move supplies to demand centers. However, we found no exceptional challenges in building to serve likely new demand for natural gas pipelines.

Models Used to Generate Results

The reference scenario for each of the TS&D systems was the Reference case from AEO2014 (EIA, 2014a). We did not use NEMS; reference cases were model runs that mimicked the AEO2014 Reference case; we did not compare any runs directly to AEO2014 NEMS runs. Table A.1 summarizes the models that were used to generate results. We did not work with any of the models directly but rather submitted requests for specific runs to the EPSA staff, who then relayed our requests to the modelers.

Table A.1
Models Used to Generate Results

Model	Description
ORNL TRIM	The ORNL TRIM LP model is an international energy and trade model that incorporates detailed information on crude production, refineries, and the transport infrastructure in the United States.
Ponderosa Crude Flow Model	The Ponderosa model is an LP model owned and developed by Ponderosa Advisors. It integrates well-level production data, rig activity, type curves, and gallons per 1,000 cubic feet–based NGL production breakouts to calculate internal rate of return and breakeven costs for wells across the United States. Granular assessment of initial production rates, decline curves, and costs make the analysis scalable to allow the study of a region, basin, field, geographic formation, crude quality, or producer. Ponderosa tracks approximately 250 areas in the United States and maintains detailed forecasts and financial metrics for each. An important feature of this model is its ability to calculate the economics based on integrated oil, natural gas, and NGL commodity revenue and producing streams. When Ponderosa forecasts the production, it forecasts the whole well and applies expectations of drilling activity to each of the hydrocarbon streams. The result is clear understanding of the impact that changing prices and costs have on overall well economics and marginal costs of production across the country (Ponderosa Advisors, undated).
ReEDS	"ReEDS is a long-term capacity-expansion model for the deployment of electric power generation technologies and transmission infrastructure throughout the contiguous United States" (NREL, 2014). "To determine potential expansion of electricity generation, storage, and transmission systems throughout the contiguous United States over the next several decades, ReEDS chooses the cost-optimal mix of technologies that meet all regional electric power demand requirements, based on grid reliability (reserve) requirements, technology resource constraints, and policy constraints. This cost-minimization routine is performed for each of 23 two-year periods from 2006 to 2050. The major outputs of ReEDS include the amount of generator capacity and annual generation from each technology, storage capacity expansion, transmission capacity expansion, total electric sector costs, electricity price, fuel prices, and carbon dioxide (CO_2) emissions" (NREL, 2014).
MarketPoint World Gas model	"The World Gas Model extends the North American Gas model to account for the globalization of the gas industry by LNG technology. The World Gas Model is an integrated model of world supply, transportation, shipping, liquefaction, regasification, infrastructure, and demand. It is based on the MarketPoint/Altos World Gas Trade Model (WGTM) extension to the [North American Regional Gas] model, which resulted from the multi-client program begun in 1990 by the consulting company that predated MarketPoint/Altos. This model was able to help the initial subscribers meet their requirements for price forecasting and fundamental analysis as well as the subsequent adopters in later years. "The World Gas Model simulates local and regional interactions among resource supply, field processing, outbound pipelining, liquefaction, shipping, regasification, distribution, demand, and interfuel competition. The World Gas Model subdivides the world into major regions connected by actual and proposed marine shipping routes and pipelines. Competition with oil and coal is modeled in each consuming region, producing results that indicate what infrastructure is most likely to be constructed in the future. Markets for emission credits and their potential impact on energy markets are included" (Deloitte MarketPoint, undated).

NOTE: LP = linear programming. NGL = natural gas liquids.

Development of the RAND Low Consumption Case for Oil and Refined Products

We constructed the RAND Low Consumption case using the following assumptions regarding the transportation sector:

- We assume a much higher penetration rate of electric light-duty vehicles (LDVs), including cars and light trucks, than is found in the AEO2014 cases. In the AEO2014 Reference case, electric, plug-in electric, hybrid, and natural gas cars account for less than 10 percent of new-vehicle sales in 2030. Some sources project far greater market-share growth rates for electric vehicles (EVs) alone. We adopt the detailed model developed by Becker and Sidhu in 2009 for projections of future EV LDV sales (Becker, Sidhu, and Tenderich, 2009). We adjust their adoption curve, which is based on the Bass diffusion model of new technology adoption, for actual 2014 market penetration and sales of EVs (Bass, 1969, pp. 215–227). The resulting projection has the total number of EVs reach 2.5 million in 2020, which is consistent with the growth rate forecast in other projections. In this projection, EVs account for 62 percent of new-car sales and 28 percent of the total car stock as of 2030. For the purposes of calculation, we consider only fully electric vehicles; in the Becker and Sidhu analysis, these vehicles dominate sales and market share of AFVs by 2030.
- We adopt the same approach for light trucks, again adjusting for today's much lower penetration. In our projection, EVs account for 45 percent of new light truck sales and 16 percent of total stock in 2030.
- We assume a much higher penetration rate of compressed natural gas (CNG) and LNG freight trucks. Low natural gas prices, if they continue, will provide large incentives to convert diesel truck fleets to LNG. There is the potential for stricter fuel-efficiency and emission laws and regulations to do the same. We assume that 70 percent of new freight truck sales are CNG (for light-medium and medium trucks) or LNG (for heavy trucks) in 2030, and adopt a similar market-share growth-rate curve to that used for LDVs. In this projection, 25 percent of freight trucks use natural gas by 2030.
- We assume that, by 2030, all municipal bus fleets consume CNG. Buses make up a tiny sliver, less than 1 percent of refined-oil product consumption, so the overall results are robust to changes in this assumption.
- We assume complete conversion of rail and shipping to LNG. The working life of locomotives and ships is much longer than road vehicles, so this would be accomplished primarily by converting or choosing to replace existing stock. As with buses, rail and shipping account for a small fraction of total petroleum consumption (3.1 percent), so changes to this assumption would have only a small impact on the final results.

- We adopt the base-case projections for VMT, fuel efficiency of new cars and light trucks that run on refined-oil products, and population growth. Although VMT have been decreasing on a per capita basis for years, the Reference case projects roughly flat total VMT through 2030. There is some reason to believe that shifting demographics will continue to put downward pressure on these numbers, but we do not foresee or have a sound basis for projecting dramatic declines that would significantly move the resulting projection.

Model Output for Electricity for 2050

Figure C.1
Total U.S. Transmission Capacity, by Scenario, 2050

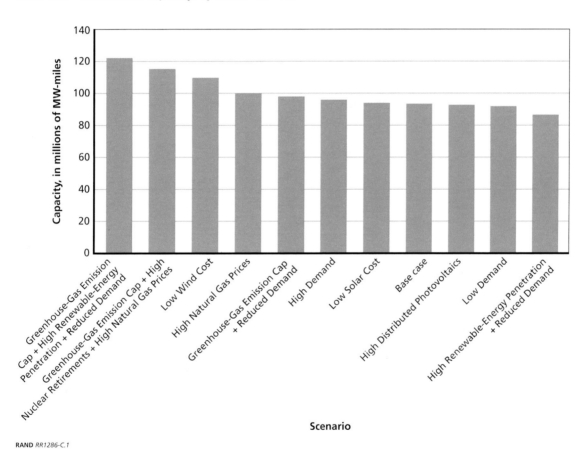

Figure C.2
Total U.S. Transmission Capacity, by Region and Scenario, 2050

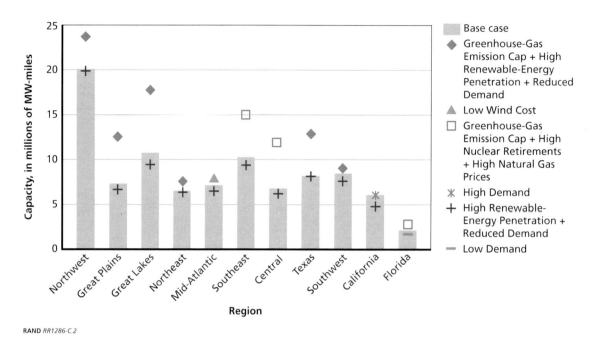

Figure C.3
Transmission Capacity Additions Under Renewable-Resource Cost Scenarios

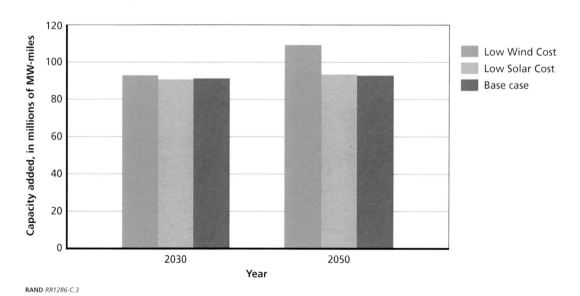

Figure C.4
Comparison of Transmission Build-Outs Between the Low Cost Wind and Low Cost Solar Scenarios,
by Region, 2050

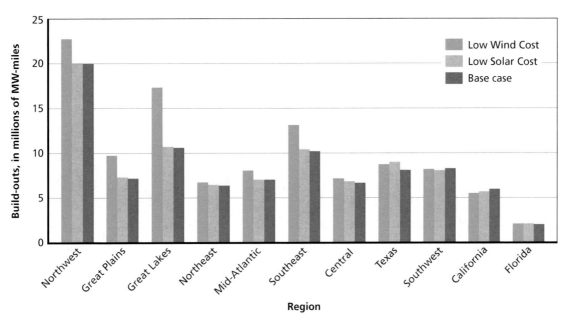

Figure C.5
Comparison of Average Electricity Prices Across All Scenarios, 2050

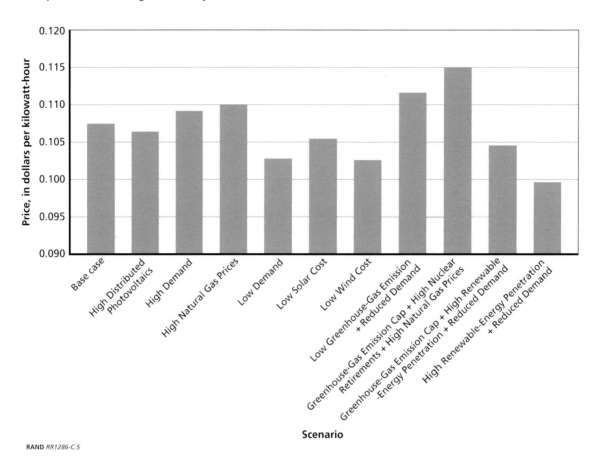

Bibliography

AEO2014—*See* U.S. Energy Information Administration, 2014a.

American Fuel and Petrochemical Manufacturers, *AFPM United States Refining and Storage Capacity Report*, Washington, D.C., January 1, 2012. As of September 22, 2015:
https://www.afpm.org/uploadedFiles/Content/Publications/Statistics/2012%20Refining%20Capacity%20Report.pdf

Andrews, Anthony, and Robert Pirog, *The Strategic Petroleum Reserve: Authorization, Operation, and Drawdown Policy*, Washington, D.C.: Congressional Research Service, R42460, June 18, 2012. As of September 22, 2015:
https://www.fas.org/sgp/crs/misc/R42460.pdf

Association of American Railroads, *Moving Crude Oil by Rail*, December 2013.

Bass, Frank M., "A New Product Growth for Model Consumer Durables," *Management Science*, Vol. 15, No. 5, January 1969, pp. 215–227.

Becker, Thomas A., Ikhlaq Sidhu, and Burghardt Tenderich, *Electric Vehicles in the United States: A New Model with Forecasts to 2030*, Berkeley, Calif.: Center for Entrepreneurship and Technology, Technical Brief 2009.1.v.2.0, August 24, 2009.

Black and Veatch, *Cost Report: Cost and Performance Data for Power Generation Technologies*, prepared for the National Renewable Energy Laboratory, February 2012.

Block, David, and John Harrison, *Electric Vehicle Sales and Future Projections*, Orlando, Fla.: Electric Vehicle Transportation Center, EVTC-RR-01-14, January 2014. As of September 22, 2015:
http://evtc.fsec.ucf.edu/reports/EVTC-RR-01-14.pdf

California Public Utilities Commission, *Order Instituting Rulemaking Pursuant to Assembly Bill 2514 to Consider the Adoption of Procurement Targets for Viable and Cost-Effective Energy Storage Systems*, Decision 13-10-040, October 17, 2013.

Carroll, Rory, "Exclusive: California Getting More Bakken Crude by Barge Than Rail," Reuters, October 23, 2014. As of November 15, 2014:
http://www.reuters.com/article/2014/10/23/us-california-bakken-barge-idUSKCN0IC17L20141023

Center on Global Energy Policy, Columbia University School of International and Public Affairs, "Summary of the Roundtable on the Resilience of the Liquid Fuel Supply Chain in the New York City Area," May 28, 2014. As of September 27, 2015:
http://energypolicy.columbia.edu/on-the-record/summary-roundtable-resilience-liquid-fuel-supply-chain-new-york-area

Chang, Judy, Johannes Pfeifenberg, and Michael Hagerty, *Trends and Benefits of Transmission Investments: Identifying and Analyzing Value*, presentation to Canadian Electricity Association Transmission Council, Ottawa, Canada, September 26, 2013. As of February 19, 2015:
http://www.brattle.com/system/publications/pdfs/000/004/944/original/Trends_and_Benefits_of_Transmission_Investments_Chang_Pfeifenberger_Hagerty_CEA_Sep_26_2013.pdf

City of New York, Office of Recovery and Resilience, Special Initiative for Recovery and Resilience, "Liquid Fuels," in *A Stronger, More Resilient New York*, June 11, 2013, pp. 131–142. As of September 22, 2015: http://www.nyc.gov/html/sirr/html/report/report.shtml

Cooper, Adam, Lisa Wood, Ingrid Rohmund, David Costenaro, and Anthony Duer, *Forecast of On-Road Electric Transportation in the U.S. (2010–2035)*, Washington, D.C.: Innovation Electricity Efficiency white paper, April 2013. As of September 22, 2015: http://www.edisonfoundation.net/iei/Documents/ IEE_OnRoadElectricTransportationForecast_0413_FINAL.pdf

Council of Economic Advisers and U.S. Department of Energy Office of Electricity Delivery and Energy Reliability, *Economic Benefits of Increasing Electric Grid Resilience to Weather Outages*, Washington, D.C.: Executive Office of the President, August 2013. As of September 22, 2015: http://energy.gov/sites/prod/files/2013/08/f2/Grid%20Resiliency%20Report_FINAL.pdf

Crane, Keith, Andreas Goldthau, Michael Toman, Thomas Light, Stuart E. Johnson, Alireza Nader, Angel Rabasa, and Harun Dogo, *Imported Oil and U.S. National Security*, Santa Monica, Calif.: RAND Corporation, MG-838-USCC, 2009. As of October 20, 2015: http://www.rand.org/pubs/monographs/MG838.html

Curtis, Trisha, Matt Calderon, Ben Montalbano, and Lucian Pugliaresi, "Lagging Pipelines Create US Gulf Light Sweet Crude Glut," *Oil and Gas Journal*, Vol. 112, No. 3, March 3, 2014. As of October 14, 2015: http://www.ogj.com/articles/print/volume-112/issue-3/transportation/ lagging-pipelines-create-us-gulf-light-sweet-crude-glut.html

Davies, Phil, "Busting Bottlenecks in the Bakken," *fedgazette*, April 23, 2013. As of September 22, 2015: https://www.minneapolisfed.org/publications/fedgazette/busting-bottlenecks-in-the-bakken

Deloitte MarketPoint, "Natural Gas Models," undated. As of October 16, 2015: https://www.deloittemarketpoint.com/industries/natural-gas/world-gas-model

EIA—*See* U.S. Energy Information Administration.

Electric Power Research Institute, *Enhancing Distribution Resiliency: Opportunities for Applying Innovative Technologies*, Palo Alto, Calif., January 2013. As of February 19, 2015: http://www.epri.com/abstracts/Pages/ProductAbstract.aspx?ProductId=000000000001026889

Enbridge, "Sandpiper Pipeline Project: Beaver Lodge Station, North Dakota to Superior, Wisconsin," undated. As of November 1, 2014: http://www.enbridge.com/~/media/www/Site%20Documents/Delivering%20Energy/Projects/Sandpiper/ ENB2013-Sandpiper-L19.pdf

EPA—*See* U.S. Environmental Protection Agency.

Farber-DeAnda, Mindi, Biofuels and Emerging Technologies Team, Office of Petroleum, Natural Gas, and Biofuels Analysis, "EIA's Crude-by-Rail Data," briefing for U.S. Energy Information Administration Energy Conference, Washington, D.C.: U.S. Energy Information Administration, June 16, 2015. As of November 2, 2015: http://www.eia.gov/conference/2015/pdf/presentations/farber.pdf

Federal Energy Regulatory Commission, "Technical Conference on Environmental Regulations and Electric Reliability, Wholesale Electricity Markets, and Energy Infrastructure: Supplemental Notice of Technical Conferences," *Federal Register*, Vol. 80, No. 36, February 24, 2015, p. 9716. As of September 22, 2015: http://www.gpo.gov/fdsys/pkg/FR-2015-02-24/pdf/2015-03642.pdf

Federal Highway Administration, Policy and Governmental Affairs, Office of Highway Policy Information, "Travel Monitoring," *Traffic Volume Trends*, December 2014. As of February 19, 2015: http://www.fhwa.dot.gov/policyinformation/travel_monitoring/14dectvt/

Flynn, Stephen E., and Sean P. Burke, *Powering America's Energy Resilience: A Report by the Center for National Policy*, Center for National Policy, May 2012.

Frittelli, John, Paul W. Parfomak, Jonathan L. Ramseur, Anthony Andrews, Robert Pirog, and Michael Ratner, *U.S. Rail Transportation of Crude Oil: Background and Issues for Congress*, Washington, D.C.: Congressional Research Service Report R43390, May 5, 2014.

Gilmour, Jared, "Train Delayed Again? Blame the Oil Boom," *Christian Science Monitor*, August 27, 2014. As of September 22, 2015:
http://www.csmonitor.com/Environment/Energy-Voices/2014/0827/Train-delayed-again-Blame-the-oil-boom

González, Ángel, "Oil Trains Crowd Out Grain Shipments to NW Ports," *Seattle Times*, July 26, 2014. As of September 22, 2015:
http://www.seattletimes.com/business/oil-trains-crowd-out-grain-shipments-to-nw-ports/

GridWise Alliance, *Improving Electric Grid Reliability and Resilience: Lessons Learned from Superstorm Sandy and Other Extreme Events*, June 2013. As of February 19, 2015:
http://www.gridwise.org/documents/ImprovingElectricGridReliabilityandResilience_6_6_13webFINAL.pdf

Guo, Christopher, Craig Bond, and Anu Narayanan, *The Adoption of New Smart-Grid Technologies: Incentives, Outcomes, and Opportunities*, Santa Monica, Calif.: RAND Corporation, RR-717-EMKF, 2015. As of October 20, 2015:
http://www.rand.org/pubs/research_reports/RR717.html

Hall, Douglas G., Richard T. Hunt, Kelly S. Reeves, and Greg R. Carroll, *Estimation of Economic Parameters of U.S. Hydropower Resources*, Idaho Falls, Idaho: Idaho National Engineering and Environmental Laboratory, June 2003. As of May 28, 2015:
http://www1.eere.energy.gov/water/pdfs/doewater-00662.pdf

Hamilton, James D., *Historical Oil Shocks*, Cambridge, Mass.: National Bureau of Economic Research, Working Paper 16790, February 2011. As of September 22, 2015:
http://www.nber.org/papers/w16790

Hempling, Scott, *Regulating Public Utility Performance: The Law of Market Structure, Pricing, and Jurisdiction*, American Bar Association, Section of Environment, Energy, and Resources, 2013.

Hines, Paul, Jay Apt, and Sarosh Talukdar, "Large Blackouts in North America: Historical Trends and Policy Implications," *Energy Policy*, Vol. 37, No. 12, December 2009, pp. 5249–5259.

Honorable, Colette D., president, National Association of Regulatory Utility Commissioners, testimony before the U.S. Senate Committee on Energy and Natural Resources, hearing on "Keeping the Lights On: Are We Doing Enough to Ensure Reliability and Security of the U.S. Electric Grid?" April 10, 2014. As of September 22, 2015:
http://www.energy.senate.gov/public/index.cfm/files/serve?File_id=57981b78-2049-457b-99cd-26f7a072ed18

IHS, *Unleashing the Supply Chain: Assessing the Economic Impact of a US Crude Oil Free Trade Policy*, Englewood, Colo., March 2015. As of June 5, 2015:
https://www.ihs.com/Info/0315/crude-oil-supply-chain.html

IHS Global, *Oil and Natural Gas Transportation and Storage Infrastructure: Status, Trends, and Economic Benefits*, American Petroleum Institute, December 2013. As of September 22, 2015:
http://www.api.org/-/media/Files/Policy/SOAE-2014/API-Infrastructure-Investment-Study.pdf

International Atomic Energy Agency, "Interfacing Nuclear Power Plants with the Electric Grid: The Need for Reliability amid Complexity," *Nuclear Technology Review 2009*, supplement, c. 2009. As of February 19, 2015:
https://www.iaea.org/About/Policy/GC/GC53/GC53InfDocuments/English/gc53inf-3-att5_en.pdf

Lempert, Robert J., Steven W. Popper, and Steven C. Bankes, *Shaping the Next One Hundred Years: New Methods of Quantitative, Long-Term Policy Analysis*, Santa Monica, Calif.: RAND Corporation, MR-1626-RPC, 2003. As of September 22, 2015:
http://www.rand.org/pubs/monograph_reports/MR1626.html

Lemphers, Nathan, "Moving Oilsands to Market: By Pipeline or Rail?" Pembina Institute, May 23, 2013. As of September 22, 2015:
http://www.pembina.org/blog/732

McCahill, Chris, "Per Capita VMT Drops for Ninth Straight Year; DOTs Taking Notice," State Smart Transportation Initiative, February 24, 2014. As of February 19, 2015:
http://www.ssti.us/2014/02/vmt-drops-ninth-year-dots-taking-notice/

Meade, Charles, and Roger C. Molander, *Considering the Effects of a Catastrophic Terrorist Attack*, Santa Monica, Calif.: RAND Corporation, TR-391-CTRMP, 2006. As of September 22, 2015:
http://www.rand.org/pubs/technical_reports/TR391.html

Montalbano, Ben, *Summary of Findings and Assumptions for QER Modeling*, Washington, D.C.: Energy Policy Research Foundation, September 18, 2014.

Narayanan, Anu, and M. Granger Morgan, "Sustaining Critical Social Services During Extended Regional Power Blackouts," *Risk Analysis*, Vol. 32, No. 7, July 2012, pp. 1183–1193.

National Economic Research Associates Economic Consulting, *Potential Energy Impacts of the EPA Proposed Clean Power Plan*, American Coalition for Clean Coal Electricity, American Fuel and Petrochemical Manufacturers, Association of American Railroads, American Farm Bureau Federation, Electric Reliability Coordinating Council, Consumer Energy Alliance, and National Mining Association, October 2014. As of February 19, 2015:
http://americaspower.org/sites/default/files/NERA_CPP%20Report_Final_Oct%202014.pdf

National Renewable Energy Laboratory, *Renewable Electricity Futures Study*, M. M. Hand, S. Baldwin, E. DeMeo, J. M. Reilly, Trieu Mai, D. Arent, G. Porro, M. Meshek, and Debra Sandor, eds., Golden, Colo.: National Renewable Energy Laboratory, NREL/TP-6A20-52409, 2012. As of June 1, 2015:
http://www.nrel.gov/analysis/re_futures/

———, "ReEDS: Regional Energy Deployment System," last updated July 23, 2014. As of June 1, 2015:
http://www.nrel.gov/analysis/reeds/description.html

———, "Annual Technology Baseline and Standard Scenarios," last updated July 17, 2015. As of June 1, 2015:
http://www.nrel.gov/analysis/data_tech_baseline.html

National Research Council of the National Academies, Committee on Enhancing the Robustness and Resilience of Future Electrical Transmission and Distribution in the United States to Terrorist Attack, Board on Energy and Environmental Systems, Division on Engineering and Physical Sciences, *Terrorism and the Electric Power Delivery System*, Washington, D.C.: National Academies Press, 2012. As of September 22, 2015:
http://www.nap.edu/catalog/12050/terrorism-and-the-electric-power-delivery-system

"Natural Gas to Exit Appalachia on Reversed Mainline Pipes, NGI Reports," *BusinessWire*, March 13, 2014. As of February 19, 2015:
http://www.businesswire.com/news/home/20140313005896/en/
Natural-Gas-Exit-Appalachia-Reversed-Mainline-Pipes

Nelson, James, Josiah Johnston, Ana Mileva, Matthias Fripp, Ian Hoffman, Autumn Petros-Good, Christian Blanco, and Daniel M. Kammen, "High-Resolution Modeling of the Western North American Power System Demonstrates Low-Cost and Low-Carbon Futures," *Energy Policy*, Vol. 43, April 2012, pp. 436–447.

North American Electric Reliability Corporation, *Grid Security Exercise (GridEx II): After-Action Report*, March 2014.

North Dakota Industrial Commission, Department of Mineral Resources, Oil and Gas Division, "North Dakota Annual Oil Production," undated. As of November 1, 2014:
https://www.dmr.nd.gov/oilgas/stats/annualprod.pdf

Nuclear Regulatory Commission, "Long-Term Cooling and Unattended Water Makeup of Spent Fuel Pools," *Federal Register*, Vol. 77, No. 243, December 18, 2012, pp. 74788–74798. As of February 19, 2015:
http://www.gpo.gov/fdsys/pkg/FR-2012-12-18/html/2012-30452.htm

Ortiz, David S., Constantine Samaras, and Edmundo Molina-Perez, *The Industrial Base for Carbon Dioxide Storage: Status and Prospects*, Santa Monica, Calif.: RAND Corporation, TR-1300-NETL, 2013. As of September 22, 2015:
http://www.rand.org/pubs/technical_reports/TR1300.html

Platts, *New Crudes, New Markets*, New York, March 2013. As of September 22, 2015:
https://www.platts.com/IM.Platts.Content/InsightAnalysis/IndustrySolutionPapers/NewCrudesNewMarkets.pdf

Ponderosa Advisors, "Ponderosa Energy: Integrated Analytics," undated. As of October 17, 2015:
http://ponderosa-advisors.com/PonderosaEnergy.html

Public Law 66-261, Merchant Marine Act of 1920, June 1920.

Public Law 109-58, Energy Policy Act of 2005, August 8, 2005. As of October 15, 2015:
http://www.gpo.gov/fdsys/pkg/PLAW-109publ58/html/PLAW-109publ58.htm

RAND Corporation, "Futures Methodologies," undated (a). As of February 19, 2015:
http://www.rand.org/pardee/pubs/futures_method/scenario_discovery.html

———, "RDMlab: Robust Decision Making for Good Decisions Without Predictions," undated (b). As of
October 15, 2015:
http://www.rand.org/methods/rdmlab.html

RBN Energy, *Pipeline and Rail Competition for Crude Transportation in North Dakota*, presentation for the
Natural Gas Energy Association of Oklahoma, January 9, 2014. As of September 22, 2015:
http://www.ngeao.org/assets/presentations/presentation-sandy-fielden-ngeao-01-08-14.pdf

Renshaw, Jarrett, and Nia Williams, "Exclusive: BNSF Puts Moratorium on Adding More Oil Tank Cars—
Sources," Reuters, New York, November 12, 2014. As of September 22, 2015:
http://www.reuters.com/article/2014/11/12/
uk-railways-crude-bnsf-eases-congestion-idUSKCN0IW2D320141112

Royal Academy of Engineering, *Extreme Space Weather: Impacts on Engineered Systems and Infrastructure*,
London, UK, February 2013. As of June 5, 2015:
http://www.raeng.org.uk/spaceweather

Short, Walter, Patrick Sullivan, Trieu Mai, Matthew Mowers, Caroline Uriarte, Nate Blair, Donna Heimiller,
and Andrew Martinez, *Regional Energy Deployment System (ReEDS)*, Golden, Colo.: National Renewable
Energy Laboratory, NREL/TP-6A20-46534, November 2011. As of May 27, 2015:
http://www.nrel.gov/analysis/reeds/pdfs/reeds_documentation.pdf

Sill, Keith, "The Macroeconomics of Oil Shocks," *Business Review*, first quarter 2007, pp. 21–31.

Snyder, Jim, "Oil-by-Rail Safety Rule Seen Adding Costs: Railroads, API," *Bloomberg*, September 30, 2014. As
of September 22, 2015:
http://www.bloomberg.com/news/articles/2014-09-30/oil-by-rail-safety-rule-seen-adding-costs-railroads-api

Sobczak, Blake, "Transport: Rail Delays Put East Coast Refining 'in Jeopardy'—Delta Subsidiary," E&E
Publishing, October 30, 2014. As of February 19, 2015:
http://www.eenews.net/stories/1060008119

Steffy, Loren, "Waiting on a (Crude) Train: The Cost of Exports?" *Forbes*, May 15, 2014. As of September 22,
2015:
http://www.forbes.com/sites/lorensteffy/2014/05/15/waiting-on-a-crude-train-the-cost-of-exports/

Tobin, James, U.S. Energy Information Administration, Office of Oil and Gas, "Major Changes in Natural
Gas Pipeline Transportation Capacity, 1998–2008," briefing, November 2008. As of October 14, 2015:
http://www.eia.gov/pub/oil_gas/natural_gas/analysis_publications/ngpipeline/comparemapm.pps

U.S. Census Bureau, "2012 National Population Projections: Summary Tables," last revised December 18,
2012. As of November 1, 2014:
https://www.census.gov/population/projections/data/national/2012/summarytables.html

———, *Annual Estimates of the Resident Population for the United States, Regions, States, and Puerto Rico:
April 1, 2010 to July 1, 2013 (NST-EST2013-01)*, December 2013. As of November 1, 2014:
http://www.census.gov/popest/data/state/totals/2013/

U.S. Department of Energy, Office of Fossil Energy, "SPR Quick Facts and FAQs," undated. As of
October 15, 2015:
http://energy.gov/fe/services/petroleum-reserves/strategic-petroleum-reserve/spr-quick-facts-and-faqs

———, Office of Energy Efficiency and Renewable Energy, *20% Wind Energy by 2030: Increasing Wind
Energy's Contribution to U.S. Electricity Supply*, Washington, D.C., July 2008. As of September 22, 2015:
http://energy.gov/eere/wind/20-wind-energy-2030-increasing-wind-energys-contribution-us-electricity-supply

———, *Electric Power Annual 2010*, November 2011. As of October 16, 2015:
http://www.eia.gov/electricity/annual/archive/03482010.pdf

————, Office of Energy Efficiency and Renewable Energy, *SunShot Vision Study: February 2012 (Book)*, SunShot, Energy Efficiency and Renewable Energy (EERE), Washington, D.C., February 2012. As of September 22, 2015:
http://energy.gov/eere/sunshot/downloads/
sunshot-vision-study-february-2012-book-sunshot-energy-efficiency-renewable

————, "SPR Quick Facts and FAQs," c. 2015a.

————, "Strategic Petroleum Reserve Inventory," c. 2015b. As of February 20, 2015:
http://www.spr.doe.gov/dir/dir.html

————, *Wind Vision: A New Era for Wind Power in the United States*, March 12, 2015c. As of October 14, 2015:
http://www.energy.gov/sites/prod/files/wv_executive_summary_overview_and_key_chapter_findings_final.pdf

U.S. Department of Homeland Security, "Secretary Napolitano Issues Temporary, Blanket Jones Act Waiver," press release, November 2, 2012. As of February 19, 2015:
http://www.dhs.gov/news/2012/11/02/secretary-napolitano-issues-temporary-blanket-jones-act-waiver

U.S. Energy Information Administration, "PADD Regions Enable Regional Analysis of Petroleum Product Supply and Movements," undated. As of September 23, 2015:
http://www.eia.gov/todayinenergy/detail.cfm?id=4890

————, *New York/New Jersey Intra Harbor Petroleum Supplies Following Hurricane Sandy: Summary of Impacts Through November 13, 2012*, Washington, D.C., November 21, 2012. As of September 22, 2015:
http://www.eia.gov/special/disruptions/hurricane/sandy/petroleum_terminal_survey.cfm

————, *Updated Capital Cost Estimates for Utility Scale Electricity Generating Plants*, Washington, D.C., April 2013a. As of October 22, 2015:
http://www.eia.gov/forecasts/capitalcost/pdf/updated_capcost.pdf

————, "Rail Delivery of U.S. Oil and Petroleum Products Continues to Increase, but Pace Slows," Washington, D.C., July 2013b. As of February 19, 2015:
http://www.eia.gov/todayinenergy/detail.cfm?id=12031

————, "Form EIA-860 Detailed Data," December 2013c. As of September 24, 2015:
http://www.eia.gov/electricity/data/eia860/

————, "Natural Gas Gross Withdrawals and Production," release date December 31, 2013d.

————, *Annual Energy Outlook 2014 with Projections to 2040*, Washington, D.C., DOE/EIA-0383(2014), April 2014a. As of September 22, 2015:
http://www.eia.gov/forecasts/aeo/pdf/0383(2014).pdf

————, "California: State Profile and Energy Estimates," updated June 19, 2014b. As of February 19, 2015:
http://www.eia.gov/state/analysis.cfm?sid=CA

————, data tables, November 2014c.

————, "Average Price of Electricity to Ultimate Customers," *Electric Power Monthly*, data for July 2015, released September 24, 2015. As of October 16, 2015:
http://www.eia.gov/electricity/monthly/epm_table_grapher.cfm?t=epmt_5_3

U.S. Environmental Protection Agency, *EPAct Section 1541(c) Boutique Fuels Report to Congress*, Washington, D.C., EPA420-R-06-901, December 2006. As of October 14, 2015:
http://www.epa.gov/oms/boutique/420r06901.pdf

————, North American Electric Reliability Corporation region map, *eGRID2012*, October 8, 2015. As of October 16, 2015:
http://www2.epa.gov/energy/egrid

Willis, Henry H., and Kathleen Loa, *Measuring the Resilience of Energy Distribution Systems*, Santa Monica, Calif.: RAND Corporation, RR-883-DOE, 2015. As of September 22, 2015:
http://www.rand.org/pubs/research_reports/RR883.html